¡ESPAÑOL EN DIRECTO!

Communicative Skills for GCSE and S-Grade Spanish

Maria-Jesus Cumming

John Murray
Stevenson College Edinburgh
Bankhead Ave EDIN EH11 4DE

Pupils' Book
ISBN 0-7195-4810-1
Teachers' Resource Book
ISBN 0-7195-4811-X
Cassettes (set of three)
ISBN 0-7195-4812-8

Author's note

This is the *Pupils' Book* for **¡Español en Directo!**, which provides activities for individual, pair and group work to help students preparing for communicative examinations in Spanish, such as GCSE and Standard Grade. It is designed to be used with the cassette tapes containing the spoken material for the listening sections of each unit, and with the *Teachers' Resource Book*.

The *Teachers' Resource Book* contains a full introduction for teachers, photocopiable sheets of extra tasks for each unit, two complete assessment tests, one for GCSE and one for Standard Grade, both with mark schemes, a continuous assessment chart, transcripts of the listening materials and selected answers. There is also advice for candidates on how to tackle the examinations, under the title *Unos consejos útiles*.

I should like to thank my publishers for their help and support and also my colleague Sharon Muir for her help and patience during the time of writing this book. Thanks also to my family and friends in Spain who helped me to collect materials and often acted as willing guinea pigs.

¡Español en Directo! is in series with **En Direct!** by Jean-Claude Gilles, whose permission to use the original arrangement and format is gratefully acknowledged. A full list of detailed acknowledgements appears on page 96.

© Maria-Jesus Cumming 1990

First published 1990
by John Murray (Publishers) Ltd
50 Albemarle Street
London W1X 4BD

Printed and bound in Great Britain by
Butler & Tanner, Frome and London

British Library Cataloguing in Publication Data

Cumming, Maria-Jesus
    Espanol en directo.
    1. Spanish. Language
    I. Title
    460

    ISBN 0-7195-4810-1

CONTENTS

BASIC Listening 1

Personal background, daily routine

1 Your Spanish class has a correspondence exchange with a class in a Spanish school. Today you have received a cassette from the Spanish pupils, telling you about themselves. Listen to the cassette and note down as much information as you can about them, in English. You will hear the recording twice.

A grid like the one here will help.

	Age	House/Flat	Brothers/sisters	Pets	Likes	Dislikes
Ana						
Isidoro						
César						
Tere						
Maribel						
Patricio						

2 A Spanish boy is describing his home town. Listen to the recording, which you will hear twice, and answer the following questions in English.

1 Where does he live?

2 How big is the town?

3 What is there to see?

4 What is there to do?

5 Why does he like the town?

3 Listen to what Estela, Juan, Belén and Eduardo say about themselves. The recording will be repeated. Make a note, in English, of what each of them says. Then write down three things that they all have in common.

Estela

Juan

Belén

Eduardo

Things they have in common :

4

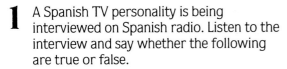

1 A Spanish TV personality is being interviewed on Spanish radio. Listen to the interview and say whether the following are true or false.

 1 Her father is a postman and she has 5 brothers and sisters.

 2 In real life she is quite similar to the character she plays on TV.

 3 She likes going to the beach in Marbella when she has the time.

 4 She usually spends her free time out with her friends.

 5 Alfonso Paz is her boyfriend.

 6 In the future she would like to have a big part in a film.

2 A Spanish assistant is comparing everyday life in Spain and in Britain, based on her personal experience. Listen to the recording and list, in English, the differences between the two countries that she mentions.

Use these headings to help you:

Daily life
Housing
Food
Schools
People

1
BASIC
Speaking

1 The new Spanish assistant has just arrived and he/she wants to know something about you. First practise with a partner, asking each other the following questions:

— ¿Cómo te llamas?

— ¿Cuándo es tu cumpleaños?

— ¿Cuántos años tienes?

— ¿Dónde vives?

— ¿Tienes hermanos/hermanas?

— ¿Cuántos años tienen?

— ¿Qué hacen tus padres?

2 Before doing this exercise, every member of the class must bring a photo of his/her family. Working in pairs, ask each other questions to find out as much as possible about the people in your partner's picture.

3 *¿Quién soy?*
Think up an identity for yourself. You can choose to be someone else in your class, your favourite pop star or football player etc. Work in pairs and try to find out each other's identity. Take turns in asking and answering questions. Here are some questions you may want to ask:

— ¿Eres un chico/una chica?

— ¿Cuántos años tienes?

— ¿Dónde vives?

— ¿Estás soltero/a, casado/a?

— ¿Eres guapo/a?

— ¿Eres famoso/a?

— ¿Eres rico/a?

— ¿Eres rubio/a, moreno/a etc?

— ¿Eres profesor/político/cantante/ futbolista/deportista etc?

1 Work in pairs. One of you will be yourself (A) and the other will play the role of a Spanish person (B).

A

During an exchange visit to Spain you went to a party at the school and met some of your penfriend's teachers. You thought one of them was particularly nice, but you can't remember her name. This is what she was like:

— tall and slim

— quite young

— dark brown hair, long and straight

— big green eyes

— she was wearing jeans and a white T-shirt.

Describe her to your penfriend and find out her name.

B

You are a Spanish boy/girl. Your British exchange partner met one of your teachers yesterday at a school party and wants to know her name. Listen to your partner's description and ask questions about the teacher to find out who he/she is talking about. This is what your female teachers are like:

La Sra Ruiz Profesora de matemáticas. Alta y un poco gorda. Tiene unos 50 años. Morena, con el pelo corto y rizado. Ojos verdes. Generalmente lleva vestido o trajes de chaqueta.

La Srta de los Angeles Profesora de inglés. Delgada y baja. Pelo oscuro, largo y liso. Tiene unos 25 años. Ojos marrones. Lleva gafas. Generalmente lleva pantalones.

La Srta Martín Profesora de física y química. Alta y delgada. Bastante joven, debe tener de 20 a 25 años. Morena, con el pelo largo y liso y ojos verdes. Generalmente viste de sport, con pantalones o vaqueros.

La Sra Jiménez Profesora de historia. Es alta y delgada. Tiene 23 años. Ojos azules. Siempre viste muy elegante.

2 While talking to your Spanish friend about houses, he/she asks you what your ideal house would be like. Describe it to him/her. Work in pairs, taking turns to play each person.

1
BASIC Reading

Amigos por correspondencia

¡Hola! Soy Elena Palencia y vivo en Valladolid. Tengo 14 años. Me gustaría escribirme con chicas de mi edad	Me llamo Mari Carmen. Soy de Vitoria. Quiero escribirme con chicos o chicas, fans de Michael Jackson	Mi nombre es Alberto Roldán. Tengo 16 años y me encanta el tenis. Quiero escribirme con chicas de 14 a 17 años
Mi nombre es Luis Torrado. Vivo en Tarragona con mis padres y mis dos hermanas. Tengos 15 años y me gusta el fútbol. Quiero escribirme con chicos de mi edad	Soy Loli Gánzer. Vivo en un pueblo cerca de Salamanca. Me encanta el cine. Quiero escribirme con chicos y chicas de mi edad (15 años)	Me llamo Julián y vivo en Cáceres. Me gustaría encontrar un amigo a quien le guste coleccionar sellos, y que es mi pasión

1

1 a) How old is Elena?
  b) Who would she like to write to?

2 a) Does Luis have any brothers or sisters?
  b) What does he like?

3 a) Where does Mari live?
  b) Who would she like to write to?

4 a) What does Loli like?
  b) Where does she live?

5 a) What does Alberto like doing?
  b) Who would he like to have as penfriends?

6 a) Who is Juliàn looking for?
  b) Why?

Now choose a penfriend for yourself, explaining your choice.

2

This is the first letter from your Spanish penfriend. Note down in English what she says about herself, and note down the same information about yourself. Then write down what you have in common.

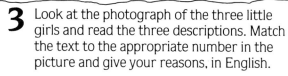

¡Hola! Me llamo Lydia y soy tu amiga por correspondencia. Tengo 15 años y vivo en Valladolid. Tengo un hermano mayor que yo y dos hermanas más pequeñas. Tengo un gato que se llama Zipi. Me gusta nadar, escuchar música y ver la Televisión. No me gustan mucho las discotecas y odio el fútbol.
La próxima vez te contaré más cosas. Escríbeme pronto. Un abrazo   Lydia

3

Look at the photograph of the three little girls and read the three descriptions. Match the text to the appropriate number in the picture and give your reasons, in English.

a) Me llamo Alicia. Tengo cuatro años y medio. Tengo el pelo corto y oscuro y ojos negros. No me gusta llevar vestidos, prefiero pantalones.

b) Me llamo Clara. Tengo cinco años. Tengo el pelo castaño y los ojos marrones. Mis colores preferidos son el blanco y el rosa. Siempre llevo vestido, no me gustan nada los pantalones.

c) Me llamo Sylvia. Tengo cinco años. Soy rubia, con pelo largo y tengo los ojos verdes. Prefiero llevar vestidos, aunque algunas veces me pongo pantalones.

1   2   3

MAS CURIOSIDADES

• Michael Jackson nació el 29 de agosto de 1959. Virgo es su signo. Mide 1,75 metros y pesa 55 kilos.

• Su libro preferido es «Peter Pan» (de nuevo el mundo de los niños); su película, lógicamente, «ET», y los instrumentos que más le gustan son los de percusión.

• Cuando está grabando en el estudio, a veces pide que apaguen las luces mientras canta. Y a menudo baila.

• Su especialísimo vestuario, con el que siempre aparece en público (cuero negro, chapas y chinchetas), forma parte de la nueva *imagen callejera* que Michael desea ofrecer.

• Le chiflan los dibujos animados. A menudo distrae su tiempo con cintas de Mickey Mouse. Palabras textuales del cantante: «Los dibujos animados son ilimitados, y si tú consigues serlo, llegas a la cumbre.» En su mansión tiene una sala de visionado de cine y vídeo con capacidad para 32 personas.

• Michael llama a Dileo *Tío Tookie,* como si se tratara de uno más de sus fantásticos e irreales amigos.

• Uno de sus mejores y más cercanos amigos (es de los pocos que le acompañan a sus habitaciones privadas) aún no ha cumplido cuatro años. Se llama Bubbles, tiene mucho de actor, derrocha fantasía y buen humor... y es ¡un chimpancé! Jugando con él, Michael se traslada a un mundo de ilusión propio del mismísimo Disney. El mundo que él más ama.

POPCORN

1 You want to write an article about Michael Jackson for your school magazine. Read what this article says about the singer and take notes in English for your own article.

Write something for all these headings:

1 *Personal details*

2 *Favourite book, film, instruments*

3 *Favourite clothes*

4 *How he spends his free time*

5 *Best friend*

---

2 Read the article about Queen Sofía of Spain and answer the following questions:

1 What does the Queen do at 10.00 a.m.?

2 What kind of work is she involved in?

3 What does she do twice a week?

4 What kind of food does the Spanish royal family prefer?

5 How do they spend the evenings?

6 What does the Queen like doing when she is in Madrid?

7 What does the article say about the way she dresses?

8 Which sports does she like?

Un día de la Reina

En una jornada típica, la Reina inicia sus actividades a las diez de la mañana, reuniéndose con sus dos secretarias en un pequeño despacho para atender a su correspondencia. Doña Sofía se ocupa personalmente de una serie de Fundaciones y Comités que preside y de los que no desea ostentar sólo honoríficamente el cargo, sino participar de un modo muy activo. Una cuestión goza de prioridad: los problemas de los niños subnormales españoles y, en general, todos los relacionados con la infancia, sin olvidar, empero, otros como la Cruz Roja y la lucha contra el cáncer. Dos veces a la semana, la Soberana recibe visitas o acompaña al Rey en las audiencias en las que se requiere su presencia. El almuerzo y la cena, en familia, son frugales, predominando los platos caseros para el Rey y las ensaladas para la Reina. La Familia Real es una familia normal que acaba su jornada ante el televisor viendo el programa de turno o una buena película de vídeo.

Algún que otro día hay tiempo para las compras, para bajar a Madrid y asistir a un buen espectáculo, preferentemente conciertos. Doña Sofía gusta de las pequeñas tiendas especializadas en productos determinados, casi artesanales. Su elegancia es proverbial, pero no le importa llevar los mismos trajes varias veces en público. La equitación y el esquí constituyen sus deportes predilectos.

1 BASIC Writing

1 Write your first letter to your Spanish penfriend, telling him/her as much as you can about yourself in Spanish. Don't forget to mention the following points:

- age
- what you look like
- your family
- your home and the place where you live
- pets (if you have any)
- your hobbies.

2 Your Spanish class is doing a survey of how people spend their free time. Copy the grid and fill it in for yourself, in Spanish.

	Lunes	Martes	Miércoles	Jueves	Sábado	Domingo
Mañana						
Tarde						

3 Your Spanish exchange partner is staying with you at the moment. Today is Saturday and you have arranged several things to do. He/she is not at home at the moment and you also have to go out. Leave him/her a note in Spanish explaining your plans for the day.

This is what you are going to do: ▷

12.30 meet friends for lunch in Pizzaland, your favourite restaurant

1.30 go shopping

4.30 go to the swimming pool

7.30 go to a party at your friend Paul's

1 Your family are planning to have a house exchange with a Spanish family for the summer holidays. Write a letter in Spanish to the Spanish family, describing what your house is like, and suggesting things to do and places to visit in your area during the time of their stay.

2 Your Spanish penfriend has asked you to send him/her an account of 'A day in the life of a British teenager' for his/her school magazine. Write about 100 words in Spanish about a day in your life. (You can make it as exciting as you like!)

3 Read the beginning of the story below and write the ending yourself. Write about 100 words.

> El lunes, Carlos se levantó a las ocho como de costumbre y después de desayunar y arreglarse rápidamente, cogió sus libros y salió de casa para ir al colegio.
> – ¡Vaya día que me espera hoy! Primero una hora de matemáticas y no he hecho los deberes y después inglés, con la profesora que me tiene manía. . .

School, jobs, future plans

1 Listen to a Spanish girl talking about the subjects she does at school. You will hear the recording twice. Draw up a timetable and fill it in, in English.

Monday	Tuesday	Wednesday	Thursday	Friday

2 Some Spanish pupils are talking about the teachers they like and dislike. You will hear their discussion twice. Listen to what they say and write down, in English, for each of them:

— the teachers they like and why

— the teachers they dislike and why.

Now write, in English, whether you agree with any of their views of teachers.

3 Four young people are describing their part-time jobs. You will hear their descriptions twice. Say which job is best and which is worst in your opinion, giving reasons (in English).

4 Four people are talking about their parents' jobs. Match the jobs below to the appropriate section (1, 2, 3 or 4) of the recording, which you will hear twice.

a) psychologist

b) painter

c) car factory worker

d) caravan salesman

e) agricultural engineer

f) housewife

g) carpenter

h) supermarket assistant

Section 1 ....

Section 2 ....

Section 3 ....

Section 4 ....

1 A teacher tells his class what rules must be observed in the classroom, but the pupils are obviously not in agreement with him. Listen to the recording and look at the picture here.

Then write down, in English, all the rules that these pupils are breaking.

El silencio es oro

2 A Spanish teacher is talking about her school. Listen to the recording and answer the questions in English.

Section 1

1 What does she say about the town of Lliria?

2 How big is the school?

3 What is the building like?

4 What facilities does it lack?

Section 2

5 What are the most popular sports in the school?

6 What do pupils write about in their news sheet?

7 In what language are some of the articles written?

8 What other groups/ clubs does she mention?

Section 3

9 How are problems dealt with at school?

10 What is the function of the 'class representative'?

11 What does the teacher think of the school?

What do *you* think of this school? Write a comment in Spanish, comparing the school in Lliria with your own and saying which one you prefer.

3 Copy the grid, then listen to what the four young Spanish people would like to be when they leave school. Fill in the grid in English.

	What they would like to be	Why	What they will need to do
Eduardo			
Mar			
Mónica			
Javier			

2

BASIC

Speaking

1 Work in pairs. Copy the questionnaire and fill it in by asking your partner questions.

Asignaturas que estudias	¿Te gusta o no? (Marca √ o X)	Profesor/a	Tus impresiones sobre la asignatura
....	☐	....	....
....	☐	....	....
....	☐	....	....
....	☐	....	....

2 Work in pairs. One of you is staying in Spain during a school exchange. Tomorrow you are going to your exchange partner's school. You want to ask your friend some questions about it first. You have made a note in Spanish of what you want to ask:

The other one of you should act as the Spanish exchange partner. Take turns to play each part.

- ¿Cuánto duran las clases?
- ¿Qué asignaturas hay mañana?
- ¿Cómo son los profes del día?
- ¿Comeremos en casa o en el colegio?
- ¿A qué hora terminan las clases?

2 HIGHER *Speaking*

1 Work in pairs. It is the Spanish assistant's birthday. You want to give him/her a present or a card. Discuss with your partner:

— what you are going to give him/her

— how much money you are going to spend

— who is going to buy it, when and where

— when you will give it to him/her.

2 You have applied for a summer job in Spain in a *colonia de vacaciones*. Before you get the job you will have to have an interview in Spanish. Practise with a partner, answering the sort of questions that you may have to answer in the interview:

— ¿Hablas bien español?

— ¿Cuánto tiempo has estudiado español?

— ¿Cuántos meses quieres trabajar?

— ¿Te gusta trabajar con gente joven?

— ¿Tienes experiencia de este tipo de trabajo?

— ¿Qué deportes practicas?

— ¿Podrías ayudar con las actividades deportivas en el trabajo?

Take turns to play each part.

3 Work in pairs. Discuss with your partner the changes that you would like to make in your school. You may wish to talk about:

— el uniforme

— el horario

— actividades después del colegio

— relaciones con los profesores.

2

BASIC *Reading*

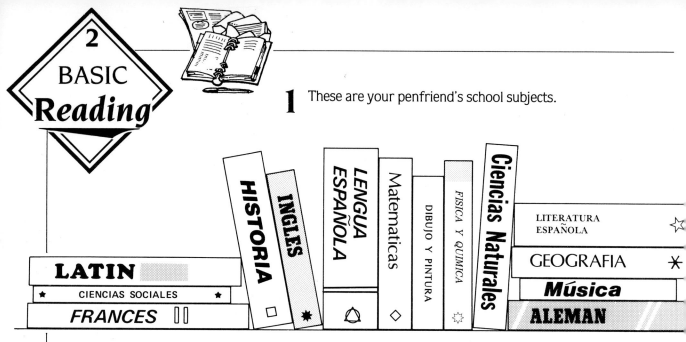

1 These are your penfriend's school subjects.

HISTORIA
INGLES
LENGUA ESPAÑOLA
Matematicas
DIBUJO Y PINTURA
FISICA Y QUIMICA
Ciencias Naturales
LITERATURA ESPAÑOLA ☆
GEOGRAFIA ✳
Música
LATIN
CIENCIAS SOCIALES
FRANCES
ALEMAN

Write down, in English, which ones are the same as yours and which ones are different.

2 A group of friends in your class are thinking of going to Spain this summer if they can find jobs. Look at the adverts and make a note in English of what is required for each job. Choose the most suitable job for each of your friends *and*, of course, yourself.

Your friends have given you these details:

AYUDANTES peluquería, 18 a 20 años. Se necesita experiencia. Llamar 437132.

CAMAREROS jóvenes, necesitamos, para restaurante de playa, zona de Benicasim. Pedimos experienca. Edad de 16 a 19 años. Damos alojamiento. Llamar de 5 a 9 tarde 9685485.

CHICA de 16 a 17 años para trabajar en zapatería. Se necesita experiencia. Llamar 4567115 a partir de 5 tarde.

CHICAS para modelos. Horario flexible. Buena presencia. Llamar de 10 a 12 mañana. 2349004.

CHICO/A de 16 a 19 años para ayudar en oficina de arquitecto. Se necesita para meses de verano. Carnet de conducir. 50000 pts al mes. Escribir Apartado de Correos 3285.

CHICA 16 a 17 años, alemán perfecto domonio. Trabajo temporal con familia. Alojamiento y manutención. Llamar 2253460, a partir de 5 tarde.

CHICO/A de 16 a 20 años, para trabajar en discoteca, fines de semana. Llamar de 9 a 15h. 8965037.

John Age 16. Have worked in a restaurant, part-time.

Sheila Age 16. Speak French and German quite well.

Alan Age 17. Have a driving licence.

Kathy Age 16. Have worked in a shop.

3 Read the postcard sent by your Spanish friend and answer the following questions.

1 Why is your friend in Palma?

2 How long is she going to be there?

3 Are the group enjoying themselves?

4 Who are the teachers accompanying the school party?

5 What did the pupils do to raise money for the trip?

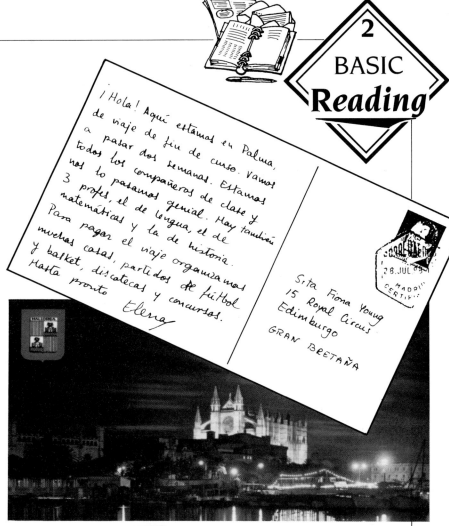

¡Hola! Aquí estamos en Palma, de viaje de fin de curso. Vamos a pasar dos semanas. Estamos todos los compañeros de clase y nos lo pasamos genial. Hay también 3 profes, el de lengua, el de matemáticas y la de historia. Para pagar el viaje organizamos muchas cosas, partidos de fútbol y basket, discotecas y concursos. Hasta pronto
Elena

Sta Fiona Young
15 Royal Circus
Edimburgo
GRAN BRETAÑA

28. JUL 93
MADRID
CERTIF.

4 You are going on the school exchange to Spain. Your Spanish partner has written to you, telling you what the school is like. Read his letter and answer the following questions:

1 What is the school like?

2 What are the teachers like?

3 What does Luis say about uniforms?

4 How is the school day organised?

5 Why does Luis think that you will like the school?

¡Hola!
Como me preguntas cómo es mi colegio te voy a contar algo.
Es un instituto, bastante grande, tiene 670 alumnos. El edificio no es muy bonito, pero los profesores son simpáticos, en general.
No tenemos uniformes, así que puedes llevar la ropa que quieras.
Las clases empiezan a las 9 y terminan a la una. Luego es la hora de comer. Puedes ir a casa o comer en el comedor del colegio. Las clases de la tarde empiezan a las tres y media y terminan a las cinco y media.
El ambiente del instituto es muy bueno y tenemos muchas actividades además de las clases. Te va a gustar.
Hasta pronto
Luis

1 You would like to go to Spain this summer and do this course. Read the leaflet and make a note in English of the following points:

1 How long the course lasts.

2 What the timetable for each day is.

3 What the accommodation is like.

SIGÜENZA
(GUADALAJARA)

CURSO INTERNACIONAL DE IDIOMAS (DE 10 A 18 AÑOS)

(Dividido en 4 secciones, según edades.)
— Español para extranjeros.
— Inglés o Francés para españoles.
● DOS PERIODOS DE 25 DIAS CADA UNO

HORARIO DE BASE:

08,30: Levantarse.
09,00: Desayuno.
09,45: Primera Clase.
10,40: Segunda Clase.
11,35: Actividades dirigidas, talleres, etc.
12,30: Tiempo libre, deportes, piscina, etc.
14,00: Comida; tiempo libre. Sobremesa.
16,00: Tercera Clase.
17,00: Actividades voluntarias, paseo, deportes, talleres, piscina, etc.
20,00: Cena; velada, juegos, etc.
23,30: Acostarse.

CLASES Y CONTACTOS CON EXTRANJEROS:

● Tres unidades diarias.
● Grupos reducidos según nivel.
● Metodología comunicativa interactiva permanente: sistema de contacto ininterrumpido con alumnos extranjeros de edad similar que participan con los españoles en todas las actividades del Curso, comparten habitaciones, mesas en el comedor, conviven en juegos, deportes, paseos, fiestas, visitas, excursiones, talleres…
● Profesores y monitores especializados, españoles y extranjeros.
● Resultados muy positivos y ampliamente probados.
● Experiencia más antigua de España en Cursos para estas edades.

ALOJAMIENTO:

COLEGIO DE LA SAGRADA FAMILIA
Villaviciosa, 2. 19250 Sigüenza. Teléf. (911) 39 07 90
Dormitorios de 8 camas. El régimen alimenticio comprende desayuno, comida, merienda y cena.

2 The inside of the leaflet gives you more information about the course. Find out:

1 What the classes are like.

2 What other activities are offered.

3 What sports facilities there are.

4 What trips are planned.

5 What it tells you about Sigüenza, the town where it is held.

SIGÜENZA (Guadalajara)

XXV CURSO INTERNACIONAL DE IDIOMAS

Fechas: 1er. Período: del 8/7 al 1/8.
2.º Período: del 3 al 27/8.

Curso de convivencia mixta españoles y extranjeros (ingleses, americanos, franceses etc.).

Contenidos

I. CLASES

3 clases diarias (español para extranjeros; inglés o francés para españoles). Utilización de vídeo.

Grupos diferentes según nivel de conocimientos.

Entrega de diplomas al final del Curso.

II. ACTIVIDADES DIVERSAS

Los alumnos participan de forma directa y responsable en su organización.

Taller de fotografía; trabajos manuales; cocina; teatro, música y canciones; montaje de veladas; disfraces...

III. ACTIVIDADES DEPORTIVAS Y RECREATIVAS

a) Deportes exteriores: fútbol, baloncesto, balonvolea, tenis, natación... Espléndido Polideportivo con canchas de juego, campos de deportes y PISCINA.

b) Deportes interiores: tenis de mesa, billar, etc.

c) Salas recreativas: futbolines, ajedrez, juegos varios de mesa, veladas...

Se organizan competiciones de deportes y juegos con activa participación del alumnado desde su organización.

Entrega de trofeos y distinciones.

Utilización de grandes espacios abiertos, campos de fuego, terreno de camping...

IV. EXCURSIONES Y VISITAS

2 excursiones de día completo a los pantanos de Buendía y Entrepeñas y al Monasterio de Piedra. Rutas campestres por los alrededores.

Recorridos culturales por Sigüenza.

Sigüenza es una vieja ciudad fortificada construida a 988 m. de altitud en la falda de una colina que domina el río Henares. Situada a 130 kms. de Madrid, en la línea férrea Madrid-Barcelona y a escasos kilómetros de la carretera nacional N-II.

Lugar pintoresco con su Alcázar, restos de la antigua muralla, Catedral y un magnífico Parador. La ciudad es toda ella monumental, declarada Conjunto Histórico-Artístico.

2 BASIC Writing

1 Your Spanish exchange partner is coming to stay with you soon. He/she wants to know which school clubs or activities he/she can join in. Write down all the possible activities, in Spanish, for each day of the week.

2 What excuse would you give for not doing your Spanish homework? Write several excuses in Spanish, and then try them out on your teacher to find out which one works best!

3 Find out how many people in your class/group have a part-time job and make a table showing this information:

Nombre	Trabajo	Horas por semana	Dinero

4 The Spanish exchange pupils are in your school. This is their programme for tomorrow. Write it in Spanish for your partner.

SPANISH PUPILS !

9.00 Meet at the school office
9.15 Go to the swimming pool in the school bus
12.00 Lunch in school
1.00 Go to classes with partner
4.00 Home with partner
7.00 School party

2 HIGHER Writing

1 Your Spanish teacher is ill in hospital and you don't like his/her replacement. Write a letter in Spanish (about 100 words), asking your teacher to come back soon and explaining why this is important to you.

2 This is what a Spanish teenager wrote about her plans for the future. Write about 100 words in Spanish about *your* plans for the future. Use the model to help you write your account.

Estoy estudiando en un instituto; si apruebo todo, sólo me quedará un año para finalizar el colegio. Luego iré a la Universidad, a estudiar una carrera, seguramente será filología; francesa o inglesa, porque me gustan mucho los idiomas y me encanta viajar a otros países, conocer gente diferente, y ver cómo viven. Los primeros años de la carrera, los estudiaré en España pero pienso que lo mejor es acabar de estudiar en el país que se hable el idioma que yo estudie, porque es la mejor manera de aprender un idioma. Cuando acabe de estudiar seguramente daré clases en algún colegio, pero lo que más me gustaría es conseguir un trabajo en un país extranjero, por dos o tres años como mínimo.

3 Your Spanish penfriend has asked you to send him/her an article in Spanish about your school for their school magazine. Write about 100 words in Spanish, describing your school.

Getting about

1 Copy the train timetables below. Listen to the station announcements, which you will hear twice, and fill in the blanks with the information given.

SALIDAS					LLEGADAS				
DESTINO	TREN	HORA	ANDEN	VIA	PROCEDENCIA	TREN	HORA	ANDEN	VIA
	Talgo		2	1	AVILA				2
						Expreso	14 23		

2 Listen to the airport announcements, which are given twice, and say whether the following statements are true or false.

1 If you wanted to catch the plane for Zurich you would have to hurry up.

2 Passengers for the Swissair flight have to embark at gate number 7.

3 Iberia flight number 453 is leaving for London.

4 Passengers for Buenos Aires will have to wait for an hour because of technical problems.

5 The gate for the Aerolíneas Argentinas flight is number 3.

3 Copy the map. Listen to the directions given in the recording (twice) and mark the routes on the map. Then write down what the places marked A, B and C on the map are. ▽

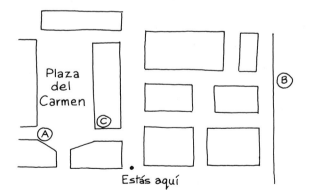

Plaza del Carmen

Estás aquí

4 Listen to the description of a room and spot the five differences between the room described in the recording and the picture here. You will hear the description twice.

1 Listen to the survey about the way people prefer to travel. Make a note, in English, of the findings for each of the people interviewed. Mention:

— which means of transport they prefer

— why.

2 *Operación Salida* is the Spanish traffic authorities' code name for the task of controlling traffic on the day when most Spanish people go away on holiday (usually at the end of July). Listen to the radio report and answer the questions in English.

1 Where is the traffic problem likely to be worst?

2 Why do the authorities expect this year to be worse?

3 What measures has the *Dirección General de Tráfico* taken to ease the problem?

4 Say what the traffic situation is in the following cities:
   a) Madrid and Barcelona
   b) Valencia
   c) Málaga.

3 Listen to the radio quiz programme *¿Conoces Madrid?*. First listen to Section 1 and write down what you have to do.

Then listen to Section 2 and find on the plan of Madrid the places mentioned by Paloma. Try to guess the mystery place before she does. Write it down when you have found it.

After doing this exercise you could try this game with a partner, using a map of your own town.

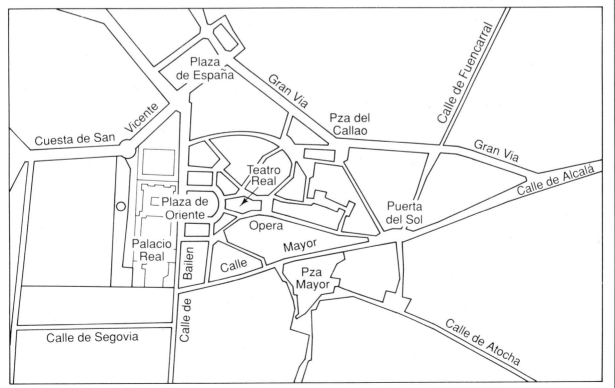

1 Work in pairs. Look at the street map and take turns in asking each other where the places numbered on the map are. Here is an example:

— Por favor, ¿Dónde está el Cine Astoria?

— El Cine Astoria está en la Avenida Dos de Mayo, cerca de la estación.

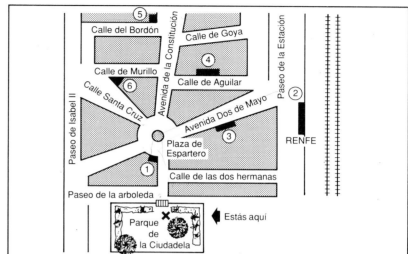

1 – Oficina de Turismo
2 – Estación (RENFE)
3 – Cine Astoria
4 – Hotel Alfonso XII
5 – Banco de Santander
6 – Museo Arqueológico

2 Work in pairs. Look at the picture of a bedroom. One of you should think of something in the picture. The other has to guess what it is by asking where it is. Take turns in asking and answering the questions. Here is an example:

A

¿Está en la pared?

¿Está cerca de la ventana?

¿Está a la derecha de la ventana?

¿Está a la izquierda de la ventana?

¿Es el reloj?

B

Sí está en la pared.

Sí, está cerca de la ventana.

No, no está a la derecha de la ventana.

Sí, está a la izquierda de la ventana.

Sí, es el reloj.

1 Work in pairs. Look at the map opposite again, and take turns in asking each other how to get to the various places marked on it. You are both in the Parque de la Ciudadela. Here is an example:

A	B
Por favor, ¿para ir al Museo Arqueológico?	Pues, mire, todo recto al salir del parque, cruce la plaza de Espartero, siga por la Avenida de la Constitución, la primera a la izquierda es la Calle de Murillo. Siga por esta calle y al final, en la esquina, está el museo.
¿Está muy lejos?	No, no está lejos. Unos 5 minutos a pie.
Muchas gracias, adiós.	De nada, adiós.

2 You meet a Spanish tourist in your town, who seems to be completely lost. He/she asks you how to get to the following places:

- a department store

- the post office

- a bank

- any interesting places to visit.

Tell him/her how to get to these places. Work in pairs, taking turns in playing the part of the tourist.

3 BASIC *Reading*

1 Write down in English the services offered in this station notice.

2 Which of the following places are on these signs?

a) a castle   f) a church

b) a swimming pool   g) a hospital

c) a market   h) a doctor's surgery

d) a supermarket   i) the town hall

e) a cinema

3 You are travelling by plane to Spain with your family. You find the following information about Barajas Airport in an in-flight magazine. Tell your parents:

1 How many cigarettes and alcoholic drinks are allowed duty-free.

2 How much money (in Spanish and foreign currency) tourists can bring into the country.

3 How to get to Madrid from the airport.

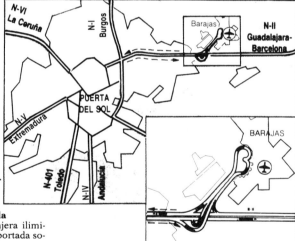

ADUANAS /

Las leyes españolas autorizan a introducir en el país los siguientes artículos:
TABACO: cigarrillos, 200 unidades - Cigarritos puros, 100 unidades - Cigarros puros, 50 unidades - Tabaco de pipa o similares, 250 gramos.
BEBIDAS ALCOHOLICAS: Con graduación igual o inferior a 22°, dos litros o un litro si es superior a 22°.
PERFUMES: 50 gramos.
AGUA DE COLONIA: Un cuarto de litro.

DIVISAS /

Importación permitida
Moneda local y extranjera ilimitada. Si la cantidad importada sobrepasa las 100.000 Ptas. en moneda local o 500.000 Ptas. en moneda extranjera. Los no residentes deben declarar esta cantidad a la entrada para evitar posibles problemas a la salida.

Exportación permitida
NO RESIDENTES
1. Moneda local hasta 100.000 Ptas. Para cantidades mayores, se debe obtener autorización de las autoridades monetarias.

2. Moneda extranjera sin límites, siempre y cuando esta cantidad no sobrepase la cantidad declarada a la llegada.

TRANSPORTES /

AUTOBUSES AMARILLOS. Destino: Plaza del Descubrimiento (antes Colón) en el Centro de la ciudad y en sentido contrario. Precio por persona y equipaje: 140 ptas. Hace paradas intermedias que podrá utilizar si sólo lleva equipaje de mano.

TAXI. A modo de orientación, un desplazamiento en taxi entre el Aeropuerto y el centro de la ciudad puede costar entre 800 y 1.000 pesetas.

1 Read the advert to find out about the cheapest way to travel around Madrid by public transport.

1 If you travel by metro
- What should you buy?
- Where?
- How much will you save?

2 If you travel by bus
- What should you buy?
- Where?
- How much will you save?

3 **Who are the** *abonos* **for?** Write down who can get them and what advantages they offer.

2 Your penfriend has sent you this letter, telling you how to get to Cerro de Alarcón, where her holiday home is, from Madrid. Take a note in English of the directions.

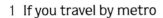

EN EL METRO

Pida en las taquillas **410 Ptas.** el billete de 10 viajes. No caduca y le cuesta un 32% menos que si viaja con billete sencillo.

EN EL AUTOBUS

Con el Bono Bus. Para que viaje 10 veces y se ahorre un 38% en relación con el billete **370 Ptas.** sencillo. Consígalo en las casetas de la E.M.T., Oficinas de la Caja de Ahorros de Madrid o Banesto.

EN TODO

Y si viaja a menudo en Tren, Autobús y Metro, elija el abono Transportes que más le convenga:

ABONO TRANSPORTES: Puede viajar sin límite, durante todo el mes, ahorrando todavía más en su gasto de Transporte Público.

ABONO JOVEN: Para menores de 18 años, un tercio más barato que el Abono Transportes Normal.

ABONO TERCERA EDAD: Por sólo 1.000 Ptas., todas las zonas, para las personas de 65 años o más.

Solicite su Tarjeta en cualquier estanco, y con ella, adquiera su cupón mensual en estancos, casetas de la E.M.T. y Metro.

	PRECIO DEL CUPÓN MENSUAL			
	Zona A	Zona B1	Zona B2	Zona B3
Abono Normal	3.000	3.500	4.000	4.500
Abono Joven	2.000	2.300	2.700	3.000
Abono 3ª Edad	1.000			

¡Hola! Te voy a explicar cómo llegar a mi chalet en la sierra. Para ir a El Cerro de Alarcón, primero, al salir de Madrid, coges la autopista M-30, dirección norte, hacia Las Rozas. Luego sigues en dirección a El Escorial; antes de llegar verás una desviación hacia Valdemorillo. Tomas esta desviación, atraviesas Valdemorillo y a la salida del pueblo hay un letrero indicando la carretera de El Cerro de Alarcón. Desde allí son sólo 5 kilómetros.
Hasta pronto Mónica

1 You have been invited to a party and you are going to take your Spanish exchange partner who is staying with you.

You have to go out, but your Spanish friend is not at home. Leave a message for him/her in Spanish, telling him/her how to get to your friend Steve's house where the party is being held. This is what you should say in your message:

▷

Go straight down to the main road, turn left, take the second street on the right. Steve's house is number 43, next to a supermarket.

2 You are going to Spain next week. This is how you are travelling:

— You are flying from London to Valencia.

— Your flight number is Iberia 436.

— You are leaving London at 9.30 a.m. and arriving in Valencia at 11.55 a.m.

Write a postcard in Spanish to your Spanish friend, telling him/her the details of your journey and asking him/her to pick you up at the airport.

1 You have received this letter from your Spanish penfriend, Pablo. He is coming to Britain with his family and he wants to come and see you.

Write a reply to Pablo in Spanish, telling him the best way to get to your house from central London. Make sure you answer all the questions in his letter.

¡Hola! Hoy te escribo para decirte que voy a ir con mis padres a Gran Bretaña y me gustaría verte. Vamos a pasar unos días en Londres y luego vamos a viajar un poco por el país.
En Londres vamos a estar en un hotel en el centro. ¿Cómo podemos ir del centro de Londres a dónde tú vives?
Mis padres piensan que podríamos alquilar un coche. ¿Es caro? ¿Es mejor viajar en coche, o en tren o autobús?
Por favor escríbeme pronto contestando a todas estas preguntas. Dame también instrucciones para llegar a tu casa.
Llegamos a Londres el 16 de julio.
Tengo muchísimas ganas de verte.
Hasta pronto

Pablo

2 Your Spanish teacher has told you about a competition organised by the Spanish railway company (RENFE) to promote travelling by rail. The prize is unlimited travel by rail in Spain for a month. To enter the competition you have to write 100-150 words in Spanish, describing the advantages of travelling by train, making use of the slogan:

RENFE
MEJORA TU TREN DE VIDA

Holidays and weather

1 Trace the map of Spain. Listen to the weather forecast, which you will hear twice, and put the appropriate symbols in the right places on the map.

2 Listen twice to two people talking about where they like to spend their holidays. Make a note of what they say about the two places, then write down in English which place you would choose. Give reasons for your choice.

3 Four people are talking about how they celebrated their birthdays. You will hear their discussion twice. Note down in English what they say, using these headings as a guide. ▽

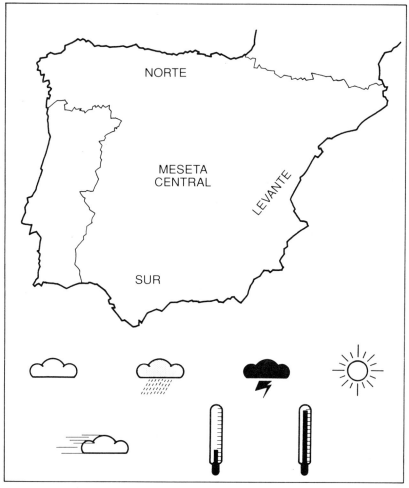

NORTE

MESETA
CENTRAL

LEVANTE

SUR

	Where	With whom	What they did	Plans for next year
Section 1				
Section 2				
Section 3				
Section 4				

1 Two girls are talking about where they are going to spend their holidays. Listen to the recording and make a note in English of the attractions of each place, the mountains and the beach.

2 Isidoro is describing how he spent his Christmas holidays. Listen to the recording and write down, in English, the differences between the ways Christmas and New Year are celebrated in Spain and in Britain.

3 Javier has just returned from a holiday, but it seems to have been a disaster. Listen to the recording and write down, in English, what went wrong with each of the following:

a) luggage

b) hotel

c) weather.

4 BASIC Speaking

1 Work in pairs. Look at this weather map for today in Spain. Take turns in asking each other what the weather is like in different parts of Spain. For example:

— ¿Qué tiempo hace en Galicia?   — En Galicia está lloviendo.

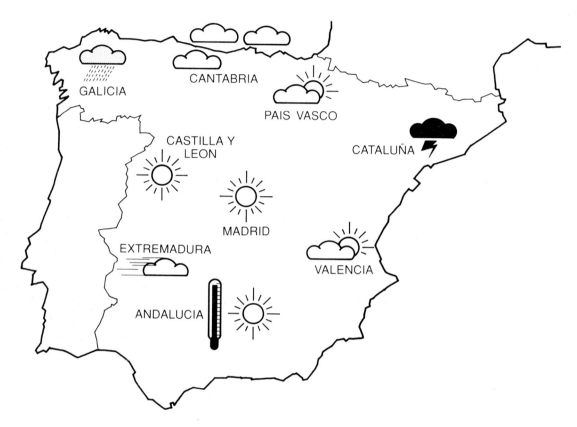

GALICIA

CANTABRIA

PAIS VASCO

CATALUÑA

CASTILLA Y LEON

MADRID

VALENCIA

EXTREMADURA

ANDALUCIA

2 Work in pairs. Take turns in asking each other what you are going to do, or what you would like to do, in your summer holidays. Here are some questions which you could ask:

— ¿Adónde vas a ir de vacaciones?

— ¿Vas con tu familia?

— ¿Cuánto tiempo vas a pasar en . . .?

— ¿Qué vas a hacer durante las vacaciones?

4 HIGHER Speaking

1 Work in pairs. Ask each other questions about your last holiday or day out. Talk about:

— where you went, and who with

— for how long

— what you did during the day/evening

— anybody that you met

— what you thought about the holiday

— whether you would like to go back or not.

2 Work in pairs. Talk about what you usually do on your birthday and about what you are planning to do on your next one. Here are some questions which you could ask:

— ¿Cómo celebras tu cumpleaños normalmente?

— ¿Prefieres tener una fiesta en casa, en una discoteca o salir con tus amigos?

— ¿Qué te regalaron para tu último cumpleaños?

— ¿Cuál fue el mejor regalo?

— ¿Cuántos años vas a cumplir este año?

— ¿Qué planes tienes para celebrarlo?

— ¿A cuánta gente vas a invitar?

— ¿Qué te gustaría recibir como regalo este año?

3 Your school has organised an exchange with a Spanish school. The pupils from the Spanish school are arriving in 2 weeks' time. You have been asked to make a short welcoming speech in Spanish about your town and the places that they can go to during their visit.

Prepare your speech and record it on cassette as a practice run.

4
BASIC
Reading

1 While planning your holiday in Spain this summer, your parents want to know whether it is possible to combine travelling by train and hired car. Read this article and make a note in English of the following points:

1 What the package offered consists of.

2 Where you can book.

3 How you will get the car and where.

4 Where you can get more information.

Reserva conjunta de tren y coche

Se trata de un billete combinado que puedes comprar, lo mismo que si fuera un billete de tren sencillo, en RENFE o en una agencia de viajes. La reserva del coche queda confirmada automáticamente, y al llegar al lugar donde viajes, a bordo del tren, te encuentras con un automóvil esperándote, llaves en mano y a tu disposición las veinticuatro horas del día. Los precios varían según la duración de la reserva. Infórmate en una oficina de RENFE.

2
1 What is unusual about these trains?

2 What does the package include?

3 Where can you get more information?

En la vida hay ocasiones en que viajar se puede convertir en todo un placer. Por cómo se viaja y por dónde se va. RENFE tiene unos trenes especialmente pensados para que Ud. disfrute del viaje y... del lugar de destino: son nuestros trenes turísticos.
Trenes con muchas ventajas y en los que Ud. tiene todo resuelto: visitas, hoteles según el tren y según el viaje. Y con unos maravillosos precios.
Con los trenes turísticos RENFE la vía es... mucho más alegre.

Infórmese en RENFE y Agencias de Viaje.

TREN DE LA FRESA • TREN MURALLAS DE AVILA
TREN DONCEL DE SIGÜENZA • TREN PLAZA MAYOR DE SALAMANCA
TREN CIUDAD MONUMENTAL DE CACERES • TREN TIERRAS DEL CID
TREN CIUDAD ENCANTADA DE CUENCA • TREN DE LA MANCHA

RENFE

IBERRAIL   **TRENES TURISTICOS**

4 BASIC Reading

3

1 What is the family relationship between Paco and Clara?

2 What does the message in the card say?

3 Why does Paco think that Father Christmas and the Three Kings will be good to Clara?

4 What is he going to do when he sees her next?

Para una sobrina muy especial

Deseo que tengas una Navidad tan alegre y encantadora como tú.

¡FELIZ NAVIDAD!

Querida Clara: Espero que Papá Noel te traiga muchos regalos. Aquí en España los Reyes Magos te van a traer muchas cosas bonitas porque me han dicho que eres muy buena. Espero verte muy pronto y tirarte del pelo que será muy largo ya.
Muchos besos de
Paco

4
HIGHER
Reading

1 Your family is renting a house in Spain this summer. The people who own the house have sent you this programme of the *Fiestas* which will take place during your stay. Write down, in English, a list of the events which you think will be worth attending for each day of the *Fiestas*.

PROGRAMA DE FIESTAS SANTIAGO APOSTOL

DOMINGO 17 DE JULIO
20,00 horas: Teatro infantil a cargo de la compañía de Angel Luis Yustas: «D. Juan Ligorio».

JUEVES 21 DE JULIO
12,00 horas: Juegos infantiles.
21,00 horas: Festival de la Escuela de Danza y Baile de la localidad.

VIERNES 22 DE JULIO
10,00 horas: Comienza campeonato de natación.
19,00 horas: Concurso de disfraces.
21,30 horas: Pregón de las fiestas a cargo de Joaquín Arozamena.
 0,00 horas: Fuegos artificiales. Bailes públicos a cargo de la orquesta BOREAL.

SABADO 23 DE JULIO
 9,00 horas: Encierro.
10,00 horas: Competiciones deportivas.
18,00 horas: Pasacalles a cargo de la Banda de Navalcarnero.
19,00 horas: Gran novillada. Con los diestros Carlos Neila y Juan Carlos Moreno. Rejoneador: Javier Mayoral. Vaquillas para los mozos. Bailes públicos a cargo de la orquesta MANDINGO. Discoteca Toc Toc, la segunda consumición, gratis.

DOMINGO 24 DE JULIO
 9,00 horas: Encierro de reses.
10,00 horas: Competiciones deportivas.
18,00 horas: Pasacalles Banda de Navalcarnero.
19,00 horas: Gran novillada con los diestros Jesús Pérez Gallego «El Madrileño» y Alejandro García García. Rejoneador: Justo Nieto. Vaquillas para los mozos.
21,00 horas: Bailes públicos. Grupo GANMA.

En Ibiza, cualquier época del año es buena para pasar unas estupendas vacaciones

En verano, la mayoría de los lugares turísticos se llenan de visitantes, pero en la isla de Ibiza se pueden pasar unas estupendas vacaciones durante los doce meses del año.

Ibiza en invierno es un mundo diferente donde se respira paz y tranquilidad. Hay muchísimas personas que desde hace muchos años pasan sus vacaciones de verano en la isla de Ibiza, pero nunca han estado allí en invierno. Si van en invierno podrán ver una Ibiza totalmente diferente. Podrán disfrutar de la isla y su belleza cuando no hay tanta gente como en verano.

En la isla, el clima en invierno es templado y agradable y se puede disfrutar del sol todos los días, dando un paseo por la playa, sentándose en la terraza de un café, mirando el mar desde el Paseo Marítimo... cualquier parte de la isla es maravillosa.

Para el que quiera divertirse, hay sitios para todos los gustos: discotecas, pubs, restaurantes, cines, conciertos y toda clase de espectáculos. Y si le gusta ir de compras podrá encontrar un surtido de productos de primera calidad a precios razonable: zapatos, cerámica, ropa, collares de perlas etc.

La isla de Ibiza es agradable en cualquier época del año. Por su clima, su paisaje y su ambiente cosmopolita. La próxima vez que piense donde pasar sus vacaciones de invierno, venga a Ibiza. No se arrepentirá.

2
1 When can you have a holiday in Ibiza?
2 What is Ibiza like in winter?
3 What advantages will the winter tourist have in Ibiza?
4 How does the article suggest that people spend their time on the island?
5 Mention three kinds of entertainment which the island offers to visitors.
6 Mention three things which the tourist can buy in Ibiza.
7 Why is Ibiza a good place for tourists?
8 What are you advised to do at the end of the article?

El arte del buen comer...

La gastronomía catalana proviene, como tantos otros aspectos, de la sabiduría y tradición popular. El tratamiento de productos sencillos consigue maravillas que el paladar agradece. Así, ha de probar el humilde pan untado con tomate, aliñado con aceite y sal, y comprobará que combina a la perfección con anchoas o con la rica variedad de embutidos del país. Pero, por otro lado, los platos catalanes llegan a un grado de inteligente elaboración y originalidad digno de las mejores cocinas. Pruebe si no el pollo con langosta, la lubina a la flor de tomillo y calabacines asados, la perdiz con uvas o el conejo con almendras, el «suquet de peix» o el «fricandó». Cada comarca catalana, en el interior o junto al mar, tiene sus especialidades. ¡Déjese aconsejar y descúbralas!

No es necesario decir que el complemento de una buena comida es un buen vino. Los excelentes vinos catalanes le ofrecen una variedad y calidad garantizadas por sus denominaciones de origen. Podrá saborear desde vinos blancos y rosados de suave paladar, hasta los vinos tintos de alta graduación y fuerte paladar. Los vinos espumosos de cava, de sabio cultivo y envejecimiento, han adquirido carta de naturaleza en Cataluña y, por su calidad, figuran entre los primeros productos de la exportación catalana. Y si es aficionado a los licores para finalizar una buena comida, también encontrará gran variedad de ellos, de elaboración casi artesanal.

3

1 Explain in English what Catalan *pan con tomate* is.

2 Mention at least four specialities of this region.

3 What are Catalan wines like?

4 How many different kinds of wine are mentioned?

5 What is the night life like in Barcelona?

6 What is special about *La Paloma*?

7 What is unusual about the casino in Peralada?

...y de pasar una noche divertida

En Barcelona la noche tiene mil colores y formas distintas, como corresponde a una ciudad cosmopolita. No obstante, en verano, algunas poblaciones turísticas ofrecen tantas o más posibilidades de diversión. Encontrará espectáculos de todo tipo, desde el más puro flamenco, a los clubs nocturnos de línea más atrevida, sin olvidar las discotecas o las cavas de jazz. La noche barcelonesa cuenta con locales insólitos y de gran interés: la sala de baile «La Paloma», con una decoración del siglo pasado y el «music hall» «El Molino», ambos con una personalidad única en su género.
Si lo desea, puede probar suerte en alguno de los tres casinos de juego, uno de ellos, el de Peralada, instalado en un antiguo castillo con valiosas obras de arte.

CATA LUNYA

4
BASIC
Writing

1 Write a Christmas card greeting in Spanish to your Spanish friend. If you need help, look at the card on page 35.

2 Your Spanish friend has sent you a programme of the day's events at his/her local *Fiesta*.

Write a programme of events for *your* local fête or carnival in Spanish to send to your friend.

3 You have just spent a weekend with your aunt and uncle who live in the country. Write a postcard in Spanish to your Spanish penfriend, telling him/her what you did during the weekend.

DIA DE SAN JUAN

10.00	Diana con bandas de música
11.00	Competiciones deportivas
17.00	Concurso de disfraces
18.00	Teatro infantil
21.00	Baile público con el grupo 'Miriada'

1 Your Spanish penfriend has written to you, telling you that she is coming to stay with you at Easter and asking you a lot of questions. Reply to her letter in Spanish, answering all her questions.

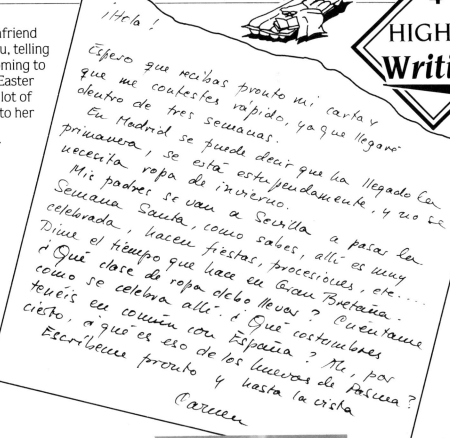

¡Hola!

Espero que recibas pronto mi carta y que me contestes rápido, ya que llegaré dentro de tres semanas.

En Madrid se puede decir que ha llegado la primavera, se está estupendamente, y no se necesita ropa de invierno.

Mis padres se van a Sevilla a pasar la Semana Santa, como sabes, allí es muy celebrada, hacen fiestas, procesiones, etc....

Dime el tiempo que hace en Gran Bretaña. ¿Qué clase de ropa debo llevar? Cuéntame como se celebra allí. ¿Qué costumbres tenéis en común con España? Mi, por cierto, ¿qué es eso de los huevos de Pascua?

Escríbeme pronto y hasta la vista.

Carmen

2 Write an article for your Spanish class magazine about a place in Britain that you would recommend to Spanish tourists for a holiday. You could write about your own town or any other place which you know well.

In your article, say something about the following:

— description of place

— monuments, points of interest

— things to do

— food

— weather

3 A Spanish magazine is running a competition. The prize is a holiday in Spain. You have to write about 100 words in Spanish about the best holiday you've ever had. Write an entry for the competition — you can make it up if you like.

Shopping

5 BASIC Listening

1 Listen twice to an advert from Spanish radio. Write down, in English, the articles which are on offer and the prices.

2 Monica went out shopping with the intention of buying these things.

Listen to the recording, which you will hear twice.

1 Which of these items did Monica actually buy?

2 Note down all the things she bought that were not on her list.

blue jersey
black trousers
shoes
something for mother

3 You are in a supermarket doing the shopping when you hear an announcement, which is given twice. Mark on your shopping list the items which are on offer and the price of each of them.

Milk
Decaffeinated coffee
Ham
Cheese
Biscuits
Bread
Fruit
Mineral Water
Wine

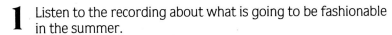
1 Listen to the recording about what is going to be fashionable in the summer.

1 Take notes in English about:

a) colours and fabric patterns

b) style of women's clothes

c) fashion for men.

2 Then look at these outfits. Explain, in English, whether they are this summer's fashion, giving reasons.

A   B   C   D

2 Eduardo wants to return a cassette to the shop. Listen to the conversation he has with the shop assistant and answer these questions in English.

1 Why is he returning the cassette?

2 Why does he not have a receipt?

3 Why is it not possible to take the cassette back?

4 What does Eduardo demand?

5 What agreement is reached in the end?

3 Listen to the recording and say whether the following statements are true or false.

Section 1

1 The girl lost the receipt for the skirt.

2 A store detective stopped her as she was leaving the shop.

3 The girl was very frightened when the detective took her to a room and asked her to show him what she had in the bag.

4 When she could not show him the receipt, he accused her of stealing the skirt.

5 He checked with the assistant who sold her the skirt.

Section 2

6 Finally, the cashier said that the girl had paid for the skirt.

7 The girl was furious, so the manageress apologised and offered her a gift.

8 She said that she could have the skirt for nothing.

5
BASIC
Speaking

1 Work in pairs. One of you will play the role of the shopkeeper in this delicatessen, the other will be a customer. Then exchange roles.

CUSTOMER

You want to buy food for a picnic.

Ask for the things you would like.

Ask how much the things cost.

Decide what and how much to buy.

SHOPKEEPER

Suggest some things.

Ask the customer how much of each.

Give the cost, then suggest some different kinds of products.

Say how well the customer has chosen.

2 While staying in Spain you want to buy some clothes. Before you go to the shop you decide to practise with your friend. Work in pairs, taking turns to play each part.

SHOP ASSISTANT

¿En qué puedo servirle?

Aquí tiene una camisa roja que está muy bien.

Sí, la hay también en verde, azul y blanco.

¿Cuál es su talla?

Sí, aquí tiene.

Sí, claro, el probador está al fondo.

Pues, ésta cuesta dos mil novecientas pesetas.

Muy bien, se la envuelvo.

CUSTOMER

You want a blouse/shirt.

Ask if they have it in other colours.

Ask for the blue one.

You are a size 40.

Ask if you can try it on.

Say that it fits, and ask how much it costs.

Say you'll take it.

Pay and say goodbye.

1 Act out a conversation taking place in each shop in the pictures. Work in pairs, taking turns to play the roles of customer and shop assistant.

(a) (b) (c) (d)

2 *¿Quién hace la compra en tu familia?*

Do a survey in Spanish. Work in groups of four. Make a note of the answers of all the members of the group. Then one of you should move to another group to find out what their answers were, and to report the answers of your group.

Here are some questions:

— ¿Cuántas veces por semana se hace la compra en tu casa?

— ¿Quién hace la compra generalmente? (¿Tu padre/madre/ hermana/hermano/tú?)

— ¿Quién decide qué cosas hay que comprar?

— ¿Tu madre es ama de casa o trabaja fuera?

— ¿Dónde hacéis la compra generalmente? (Varias tiendas, supermercado, hipermercado.)

1 Write down which of these items you could buy for breakfast and for lunch. You can have the same item in both columns if appropriate.

Breakfast	Lunch

49. Galletas de Barquillo

117. Cafés La Estrella Mezcla Exprés — MITAD NATURAL · MITAD TORREFACTO · MOLIDO

159. OROSOL ACEITES DEL SUR

169. Nesquik

99. PASTAS ALIMENTICIAS

59. TOMATE frito Alesves

79. ketchup ORLAND

109. VALDEPEÑAS LOS MOLINOS

66. valle del PAS LECHE ENTERA UHT

2 You want to buy a present for your baby sister, but you only have 1500 pesetas to spend. Look at this advert and write, in English, what you could buy for her.

Hasta el Sábado 31, UNA GRAN OFERTA.

Chandal afelpado, con estampación	~~1.525~~	**1.195**	**Pantalón** largo con peto, de pana	~~1.995~~	**1.595**	**Cuna** de madera, 120 × 60, Somier tres posiciones ~~12.995~~ **10.395**
Vestido con estampado de flores	~~4.695~~	**3.695**	**Camisa** con manga larga en viyella a cuadros	~~1.895~~	**1.495**	**Parque** de aro, tapizado ~~5.775~~ **4.595**
Vestido con estampado de cuadros	~~4.695~~	**3.695**	**Camisa** con manga larga, estampada	~~1.495~~	**1.195**	**Bota** en Box-calf, para bebé ~~1.350~~ **995**
Pantalón largo de pana	~~1.425~~	**1.095**	**Buzo** de ciré liso	~~3.995~~	**3.195**	**Bota** en Box-calf, Tallas: 1 a 3 años ~~2.795~~ **2.195**
Pantalón largo de pana	~~1.995~~	**1.595**	**Jersey** con manga larga en liso	~~1.495~~	**995**	
Pantalón largo con peto, tejano	~~1.795~~	**1.395**				

3 Your mother was given this card in Avila. She wants to know what they sell in this shop. Write down in English as many items as you can.

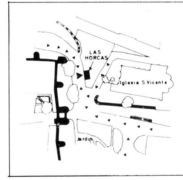

Las Horcas

RECUERDOS DE AVILA
ARTESANIA - CERAMICA
VINOS DE CEBREROS
QUESO PURO DE OVEJA
CHORIZO DE AVILA

San Vicente, 3 - Telf. 22 04 55   Avila

4 You want to buy some food for a picnic. This is your shopping list:

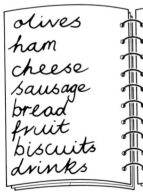

olives
ham
cheese
sausage
bread
fruit
biscuits
drinks

Write down the items on your list which you could buy in this shop. Put a tick against the items which are on offer.

1 Find out which of the following are offered by *El Corte Inglés*.

a) travel agency

b) hairdresser

c) fashion items

d) payment by credit card

e) foreign currency exchange

f) car hire

g) restaurants.

Todas sus compras, en España, sin salir de El Corte Inglés.

El Corte Inglés cuenta con 17 Grandes Centros Comerciales repartidos por toda España, dedicados a la Moda y a sus complementos, el Hogar, la Decoración, los Deportes... Pero, además cada Centro de El Corte Inglés es todo un mundo de atenciones y servicios: Agencia de Viajes, cambio de moneda extranjera, Carta de Compras, Restaurantes-Cafetería, Boutiques Internacionales, souvenirs y artículos turísticos, admisión de Tarjetas de Crédito... Todo para hacer más fáciles sus compras.

TOURISHOP
TAX FREE FOR TOURISTS
El Corte Inglés

MADRID DE COMPRAS

Horario comercial: De 9,30 13,30 y de 17,30 a 20 horas. Lo grandes almacenes (Corte Inglés Galerías Preciados) no cierran a mediodía. Los Vips permanecen abiertos hasta las 3 de la madrugada.

Comprar en comercios tradicionales: Pequeñas y variadísimas tiendas del Centro: Puerta del Sol, Plaza Mayor y sus innumerables calles vecinas.

Comprar en los clásicos Comercios «con estilo», dedicados principalmente a joyería, modas, piel y muebles. Gran Vía, Càlle del Carmen y Preciados, y las Boutiques del Barrio de Salamanca.

Comprar en los nuevos: Lo último en sus escaparates. Calle Princesa, Centro Azca y el modernísimo Centro Comercial Madrid-2 (La Vaguada), al norte de la ciudad.

Antigüedades. Existen tres zonas: El Rastro, mercado de todo, cuenta con valiosos anticuarios. Ribera de Curtidores y calles cercanas.
Barrio de Salamanca, prestigiosas tiendas diseminadas por sus calles.
Zona de Carrera de San Jerónimo, Santa Catalina y El Prado.

2 Find out about shopping in Madrid by reading this article.

1 What are the opening times of:
   a) normal shops
   b) department stores
   c) *Vips*?

2 What kind of shops can be found in the *Puerta del Sol/Plaza Mayor* area?

3 What kind of things can you buy in the 'classical shops'?

4 Where are the new shops?

5 Where can you find antiques?

3 At the end of your stay in Spain you want to buy some presents for your family. You find these gift ideas in a magazine. Choose presents for three members of your family. Write down in English what you have chosen for each, giving reasons for your choice.

Juguetes de latón

Tiernos y nostálgicos, estos juguetes te remontarán a épocas pasadas. Hay muchísimos modelos y tamaños. Los de la fotografía cuestan entre 500 y 600 pesetas.

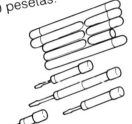

Destornillador

Destornilladores utilísimos y de todos los tamaños, hasta los más pequeños, que te servirán para cambiarle la pila al reloj o para intentar ser una «manitas» con tu batidora. Valen 1.450 pesetas.

Cubitos de playa

Gracioso cubito con el que tus pequeños disfrutarán «horrores» en la playa o en el parque. Lleva de todo: rastrillo, pala y moldes para hacer figuritas. Se divertirán y sacarán partido a su imaginación. Vale 1.100 pesetas

Antigua Casa Crespo

En Casa Crespo encontrarás las imprescindibles alpargatas de todo trote para el verano. Las hay de todos los colores, formas y tamaños, son cómodas, frescas y de plena moda. Si no conoces esta tienda, acércate por allí; te sorprenderá.

Copas de helado

Estas copas de helados en llamativos colores llevan incorporada su correspondiente cucharilla a juego. Cada una cuesta 380 pesetas

5 BASIC Writing

1 Your Spanish friend has offered to accompany you to buy presents for your family and friends before you leave Spain. In order to decide what to buy, draw up a table like this and fill it in for all the people you want a present for.

Nombre	Le gusta(n)	Posibles regalos
Papá	Fumar en pipa la música	una pipa, un encendedor un disco de flamenco

2 Tonight you are having a party for your Spanish friend who is staying with you at the moment. There are still a few things to buy, but you have to go to school now. Leave some money and write a message in Spanish for your friend, asking him/her to buy these things, and saying where to do the shopping.

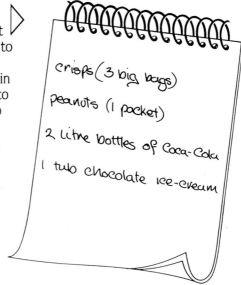

crisps (3 big bags)
peanuts (1 packet)
2 litre bottles of Coca-Cola
1 tub chocolate ice-cream

3 During your stay in Spain you decide to have a picnic with your penfriend's friends.

Write a shopping list, in Spanish, of the things you will need to buy for the picnic.

1 Your Spanish friend is coming to stay with you soon. He/she has written to you, asking what presents he/she could bring for you and your family. Write a reply in Spanish, telling your friend what presents would be suitable for everybody.

2 Your Spanish friend has sent you this letter, telling you something about shopping in Spain. ▷

Write a reply to his letter in Spanish, answering his questions and explaining differences and similarities between shopping in Spain and in Britain.

3 Write down, in Spanish, a summary of the findings of the survey in task 2 on page 43.

> A mí me encanta ir de tiendas, me gusta muchísimo ir al mercado a hacer la compra con mi madre. A pesar de que hoy día mucha gente compra en los supermercados, yo prefiero el mercado, con tantos puestos y tanto ruido. Mi madre prefiere comprar en las tiendas pequeñas del barrio, donde todo el mundo se conoce, dice que los supermercados son prácticos pero muy impersonales. Para comprarme ropa voy o bien a una boutique, o a uno de los grandes almacenes como "El Corte Inglés" o "Galerías", porque hay de todo y están abiertos todo el día, de 9 de la mañana a 8 de la tarde. Algún Domingo voy al Rastro, que es un mercado al aire libre, enorme, donde se puede comprar de todo, desde cosas de segunda mano a antigüedades, discos, libros, de todo. Se encuentra ropa bastante barata y también discos y cassettes. ¿Cómo son las tiendas por ahí? Cuéntame algo en tu próxima carta.
> Hasta la próxima.
>
> Alberto

6
BASIC
Listening

Food and drink

	Tapas	Drinks
Customer 1		
Customer 2		
Customer 3		
Customer 4		

1 Four people are ordering tapas and drinks in a bar. Imagine you are the waiter, and take down the order for each of the four customers. You will hear the orders twice.

2 Write down, in English, four good things about the restaurant that you will hear described twice.

3 You will hear an advert from Spanish radio twice. Make a note in English of what the new cafe *Alaska* is like, so that you can tell your parents.

4 Copy the grid below.

Some Spanish people are talking about the kind of food they like and dislike. You will hear their conversation twice. Write down their likes and dislikes, then tick whether you agree or disagree with them.

	Likes	Dislikes	You agree	You disagree
Section 1				
Section 2				
Section 3				
Section 4				

1 Four Spanish people are explaining what some Spanish dishes are like.

Section 1   *Ensaladilla Rusa*

Section 2   *Paella*

Section 3   *Pisto*

Section 4   *Huevos a la Flamenca*

Make a note of what they say about each dish, and write down in English which ones you would or would not like, explaining why.

2 Four people are complaining in a restaurant. Write down in English what each person's complaint is, and what the waiter is going to do about it.

3 Three Spanish people are talking about the specialities of their region. Write down in English what the specialities are, and which ones you would or would not like, giving reasons.

Region	Speciality	Would you like it?
León		
Madrid		
Andalucía		

6
BASIC
Speaking

1 Work in pairs. One of you will be the waiter/waitress, the other a customer ordering drinks for some friends. Then exchange roles.

WAITER/WAITRESS	CUSTOMER
¿Qué desean?	Ask for a cola and an orange juice.
Muy bien, ¿algo más?	Ask if they have bottles of beer.
Sí, tenemos en botellín y en botella grande.	Ask for a small bottle.
Sí, aquí tienen.	Ask how much it is.
Pues, son quinientas setenta y tres pesetas.	Pay and say thank you.

2 Work in pairs. One of you will be the customer, ordering snacks from this menu for your family. The other will be the waiter/waitress. Then exchange roles. ▷

3 You are with a group of friends in Spain. You all want something to eat and drink. You find a café and decide to order.

— 2 colas and 1 lemonade

— veal with chips and salad

— hamburger, chips, egg and salad

— chop, chips and salad.

Order for everybody from this menu.

Work in pairs, one of you acting as the waiter/waitress. Then exchange roles.

▽

TAPAS

CARNE CON TOMATE
MORCILLA
LONGANIZA Y CHORIZO
ALBONDIGAS
RACION DE PAELLA
CROQUETAS
CALAMARES
PULPO
GAMBAS
LENGUADOS
RAYA
CHIPIRONES
BOQUERONES
BOCADILLOS
CHORIZO, SALCHICHON, QUESO Y JAMON
LOMO PEPITOS
HAMBURGUESAS
ANCHOS
ATUN
LONGANIZA
CHORIZO CASERO

RACIONES Y PLATOS COMBINADOS	PTAS
1 PAELLA de MARISCOS o CARNE por PERSONA	400
2 SOPA YUSUF ESPECIALIDAD DE LA CASA	200
3 HUEVO BEICON Y PATATAS	350
4 TORTILLA FRANCESA LOMO Y PATATAS	400
5 ENTREMESES VARIADOS DE LA CASA	350
6 COMBINADO YUSUF JAMON QUESO LOMO horno	500
7 TERNERA PATATAS Y ENSALADA	550
8 HABAS CON JAMON HUEVO Y PATATAS	500
9 HUEVO JAMON PLANCHA Y PATATAS	500
10 ALBONDIGAS PATATAS Y HUEVO	00
11 HAMBURGUESA PATATAS HUEVO Y ENSALADA	400
12 CROQUETAS PATATAS Y HUEVO	600
13 PEZ ESPADA Y ENSALADA	600
14 MERLUZA FRITA O PLANCHA	600
15 CONEJO EN ADOBO	500
16 CODORNICES CON PATATAS	550
17 CHULETA PATATAS Y ENSALADA	600
18 RACION JAMON TREVELEZ O QUESO AÑEJO	

1 Your Spanish friend is treating you to a meal in a restaurant. Here are the menus from two restaurants.

Discuss with your partner the menus, prices etc, and try to agree on the restaurant that you would both like to go to.

Restaurante La Chapela

Menú del día
750 pts

Sopa de cocido
Guisantes con jamón

Chuleta de cerdo
Merluza a la Romana

Pan, vino, fruta

Bar - Restaurante Manolo

Menú del día
900 pts

Espárragos con mayonesa
Gazpacho
Ensalada mixta

• • • • • • •

Paella
Cordero asado
Pollo al ajillo

• • • • • • •

Flan
Tarta al whisky
Helados variados

Pan, vino, cerveza, café

2 Your class has been asked to send a cassette to a Spanish school, telling them about food in Britain. Prepare your talk and record it on cassette.

You could say something about the following:

— lo que comen los británicos en general

— los platos más conocidos

— lo que tú comes en un día normal

— lo que se come en ocasiones especiales (Navidades, cumpleaños etc)

— las horas de las comidas

— tu comida favorita

— las cosas que no te gustan.

3 When you have recorded your talk, work in pairs and compare what you each said for task 2. Discuss, in Spanish, what you have in common as regards likes/dislikes about food.

6
BASIC
Reading

1 Read these adverts for restaurants and answer the questions.

1 Where can you get Indian food?

2 Which restaurant is open until 1.00 a.m.?

3 Where can you get paella to take away?

4 Where can you eat French food?

5 Which restaurant specialises in seafood?

6 Which restaurant is closed on Sunday evenings?

7 Where can you get Italian food?

8 Where do they serve Moroccan food?

Restaurante Coto Real

Director

ALFREDO MENDEZ FDEZ.

ESPECIALIDADES:
Rape langostado, merluza a la sidra, salmón papillote, churrasco a la brasa, entrecot al cabrales.

Ctra. La Coruña, km. 16,900 (VINIENDO HACIA MADRID) — Tel. 637 62 29-637 75 00 — 28023 Madrid

Restaurante EL VAGON

COCINA CASERA ASTURIANA

NARVAEZ, 57
TEL. 274 22 08
274 22 07

Abierto todos los días excepto domingo noche

BAR RESTAURANTE el soto
ESPECIALIDAD EN CARNES A LA PARRILLA

MOSTOLES (MADRID)

CARNES Y PESCADOS A LA BRASA

Restaurante abierto de 1 de la tarde a 1 de la madrugada continuado

AVDA. DE LOS DEPORTES JOAQUIN BLUME, N.º 1
TEL. 618 00 30

Brummel's
RESTAURANTE CERVECERIA

COUSCOUS MARROQUI

C/ Serrano, 93 - Tel. 261 27 89
Madrid 28006

Rata Bar-Restaurante

PRIMERA CASA EN MARISCOS
COMEDORES PRIVADOS

Teléfonos:
273 10 87
273 82 98

Narváez, 68
28009
MADRID

SIVAGAMI
INDIAN RESTAURANT

LA AUTENTICA Y TRADICIONAL GASTRONOMIA DE LA INDIA

Calle San Felipe, 3
(Esq. Bravo Murillo, 288 o Infanta Mercedes, 73)

Tel.
571 28 65

Piccolo
RISTORANTE - PIZZERIA
HORNO DE LEÑA

Príncipe de Vergara, 280
Tel. 240 86 48

TABERNA ANDALUZA RESTAURANT
LA TACITA DE PLATA

PESCADITO Y PAELLA PARA LLEVAR

Fco. Silvela, 50
Alcalde Sainz de Baranda, 32

Telef. 255 40 43
Telef. 409 67 22

Restaurante LA NUEVA MAQUINA

Alta cocina asturiana. Parrilla de carbón.
Jardín-terraza. Comedores privados.

AVENIDA DEL BRASIL, 7
TELS. 455 08 73 - 455 10 02 - 456 13 26
28020 MADRID

Crêperie La Raclette

NO LE DE MAS VUELTAS
LOS MEJORES CREPES DE MADRID
ESPECIALIDADES FRANCESAS

Calle Infanta Mercedes 99 Telf 2703748   Madrid 28020

1 Your friend is thinking of going on a diet. You find these tips on dieting in a Spanish magazine. Make a note in English of the advice given about the following, in order to tell your friend.

a) bread

b) oil

c) drinks

d) green vegetables

e) salt.

MUY IMPORTANTE

— Consumir no más de 60 gramos de pan en cada comida. Mejor integral.

— El aceite se limita a 20 gramos al día, y es preferible utilizarlo crudo, como condimento.

— Beber agua y tisanas tanta como se desee, mejor entre horas y limitando la de las comidas. Prohibido el vino y otros alcoholes.

— La verdura puede ser consumida cruda o cocida, teniendo cuidado de no sazonarla demasiado. También puede —y debe— comerse al inicio de las comidas.

— Reducir al máximo el consumo de sal. Cuando se use, utilizar preferentemente sal marina o integral.

A Salsa: Bate el aceite con el zumo de limón, la mostaza y el azúcar, sazónalo con sal y pimienta.

B Preparación: 20 minutos

Ensalada de fruta

C ### INGREDIENTES

D 2 cebollas, 2 naranjas, 2 rodajas de piña, 1 pimiento verde, 12 aceitunas negras, 4 cucharadas de aceite, 3 cucharadas de zumo de limón, 1/2 cucharada de azúcar, sal, pimienta, mostaza.

E ### PREPARACION

F Mézclalo todo, aliñalo con la salsa y déjalo en el refrigerador hasta el momento de servirlo.

G Corta las cebollas y las naranjas en rodajas finas, el pimiento en tiritas y la piña en trocitos; deshuesa las aceitunas.

2 You find this recipe in a Spanish magazine, but the instructions are all mixed up. Put them in the right order.

What ingredients would you need to make this recipe? Write them down in English.

3 While staying in Madrid your parents want to go to a restaurant. You have a leaflet which lists a number of restaurants in Madrid. For five of the restaurants listed in the leaflet which appeal to you most, list

a) the type of food

b) whether credit cards accepted

c) price range

d) when it closes and any special points.

■ **TAJ MAHAL**
Plaza Conde Toreno, 2 (detrás de la plaza de España). Cocina hindú. Lunes, cerrado. Admite tarjetas. Precio medio, de 1.500 a 2.000 pesetas.

■ **AIRIÑOS DO MAR**
Orense, 39. Tel. 456 00 52. Marisquería. Especialidad en mariscos y pescados. Domingos y el mes de agosto, cerrado. Admite tarjetas.

■ **EL ACUEDUCTO**
General Alvarez de Castro, 7. Tel. 447 20 13. Cocina segoviana. Especialidad en carnes. Cierra domingos y festivos noche. Admite tarjetas.

■ **LA ALBUFERA**
Capitán Haya, 43. Tel. 279 63 74. Cocina valenciana. Especialidad en arroces y paellas. Agosto, cerrado. Admite tarjetas. Precio medio de 1.500 a 2.500 pesetas.

■ **AL-MOUNIA**
Recoletos, 5. Tel. 275 01 73. Cocina árabe. Especialidades en tallin, pinchos morunos y cordero asado. Domingo, lunes y el mes de agosto, cerrado. Admite tarjetas. Precio medio, de 4.000 a 5.000 pesetas.

■ **CASA PEPA**
Urbanización Cuesta Blanca, carretera de Burgos, km. 8,500. Tel. 653 08 78. Cocina casera. Especialidad en alubia roja y merluza a los puerros. Domingos noche y el mes de agosto, cerrado. Admite tarjetas. Precio medio, de 2.500 a 3.000 pesetas.

■ **AMALUR**
Padre Damián, 37. Tel. 457 62 98. Cocina vasca. Especialidad en lubina en salsa de langosta, merluza frita con pimientos y solomillo. D. Pedro. Sábados mediodía, domingos y el mes de agosto, cerrado. Cenas ambientadas con piano. Admite tarjetas. Precio medio de 3.500 a 4.500

■ **VILLAGARCIA**
Orense, 6. Entreplanta. Tel. 456 70 79. Cocina gallega. Especialidad en carnes y pescados. Domingos, cerrado. Precio medio, de 2.000 a 2.500 pesetas.

■ **LA PARRILLA**
Capitán Haya, 55. Tel. 279 64 51. Asador. Especialidad en chuletón de buey. Domingos y el mes de agosto, cerrado. Admite tarjetas. Precio medio, de 2.000 a 3.000 pesetas.

■ **BURDEOS**
Argensola, 7. Tel. 410 36 71. Cocina francesa. Sábados mediodía, domingos y el mes de agosto, cerrado. Admite tarjetas. Precio medio, de 2.000 a 3.000 pesetas.

■ **ARARAD**
Costa Rica, 15. Tel. 457 73 26. Cocina armenia. Especialidad en cordero asado. Domingos, cerrado. Admite tarjetas. Precio medio, de 4.000 a 5.000 pesetas.

6 BASIC Writing

1 You have just arrived in Spain and your penfriend's mother wants to make sure that you'll enjoy her cooking. She asks you to write down the things you like and dislike. List things in Spanish under these headings:

Me encanta(n)	Me gusta(n)	No me gusta(n)	No me gusta(n) nada

2 Your Spanish penfriend is staying with you. You have to go out but he/she is coming home for lunch. Leave a message for your friend in Spanish, saying what he/she can have for lunch.

This is what there is. ▷

1 Your Spanish penfriend has sent you this recipe for Spanish omelette.

Write *your* favourite recipe, in Spanish, to send to your penfriend. The terms used in this recipe should help you.

Tortilla de patatas

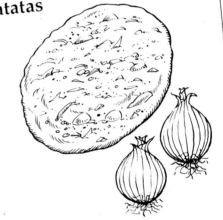

Ingredientes

4 patatas medianas
2 cebollas
5 huevos
aceite de oliva
sal

Pelar las patatas y las cebollas.
Cortarlas en rajas muy finas.
Freir las patatas y las cebollas en bastante aceite de oliva, hasta que estén blandas.
Batir los huevos.
Sacar las patatas y cebollas de la sartén y mezclarlas con los huevos.
Poner muy poco aceite en la sartén y echar la mezcla de patatas, cebolla y huevos.
Cuando la tortilla esté hecha por un lado, poner un plato encima de la sartén y dar la vuelta rápidamente.
Echar un poco de aceite en la sartén y luego echar la tortilla para hacerla por el otro lado.
Se puede comer fría o caliente.

2 You have been asked to write an article for your school magazine on the subject of Spanish food. Write your article in Spanish, so that your penfriend can comment on it before it is printed.

BASIC Listening

7

Finding accommodation

1 You are staying on a campsite in Spain with your parents. You hear an announcement, which is repeated. Make a note, in English, of the information which would be of interest to them and to you.

2 Copy the grid and listen twice to the descriptions of the three hotels. Tick the facilities offered by each of the three hotels, then decide which one you would prefer to stay in and why.

Hotel	Rooms with bath	Rooms with minibar	Rooms with terrace	Rooms with TV	Restaurant	Swimming pool	Car park
Los Arcos							
Jaime I							
Casablanca							

3 You are staying with your Spanish penfriend. Your friend's sister is looking for a flat. You hear an advert on the radio when she is out. It is repeated on the recording.

This is the list of what she wants the flat to have. Which of these features does the flat in the advert have?

a) quiet surroundings

b) lift and entryphone

c) swimming pool in the building

d) car-parking facilities

e) well-equipped kitchen

f) at least two bedrooms

g) a terrace.

1 Your penfriend's mother is telling you how she wants you to keep your bedroom during your stay in their house. The picture illustrates what your own bedroom usually looks like. Write down in English all the things that are against the rules in your friend's house.

2 A couple are discussing where to stay during their holidays. Note down in English the advantages and disadvantages of each of the two types of accommodation which are mentioned.

	Camping	Hotel
Advantages		
Disadvantages		

3 A woman arrives at a hotel to find that her room has not been booked. Listen to the conversation between the woman and the hotel receptionist, and answer the following questions in English.

1 What does the receptionist offer her?

2 Why is she not happy about this?

3 What does the receptionist suggest to please the woman?

4 The room offered does not have a bath or a television. What makes the woman take it?

5 What does the receptionist promise the woman?

7 BASIC Speaking

1 Work in pairs. One of you will play the part of a customer at a travel agent's, asking about the facilities of the *Hotel Los Molinos* in Ibiza. You want to know:

— where the hotel is

— whether all rooms have a bath

— if there is a swimming pool

— what other facilities it offers

— what the half board consists of.

The other will play the part of the travel agent, who answers the questions using this information from a brochure. Then exchange roles.

▽

H. LOS MOLINOS

2 Your family want to rent an apartment in Alicante for two weeks in September. You have to phone up to find out whether an apartment advertised is suitable or not.

Alicante Apartamento
Tel 4300451

You want to know:

— how many bedrooms there are

— if it is near the beach

— if it has a balcony

— if there is a swimming pool

— if it is available in September.

Work in pairs, one person playing the owner's agent, who answers the questions with the help of this extract. Then exchange roles. ▽

1 Your parents have asked you to phone the *Hotel Residencia Las Palmeras* in Javea, to book the family's summer holiday. When you phone, you are asked to leave a message on their answering machine.

This is what you have to say:

— You want to book a double room and two singles, all with bath/shower.

— The booking is for three weeks, starting the 25th July.

— Your parents will be sending a 10% deposit.

— You would like the hotel to write back, confirming the booking (don't forget to give your address).

— You are travelling by plane to Alicante, so you would be grateful if they could send you a timetable of buses from Alicante to Javea.

2 Work in pairs. Discuss with your partner where you prefer to stay when you are on holiday. Talk about the following:

— ventajas y desventajas de hotel, camping, apartamento/chalet, casa de amigos

— cuál prefieres tú y por qué

— dónde pasas las vacaciones normalmente.

7

BASIC
Reading

1 Your grandparents want to rent a place in Spain next summer. You find this advert in a Spanish magazine. Make a note of the information in order to tell them. They would like to know in particular: ▷

1 Where it is.

2 What accommodation it offers.

3 How well equipped the kitchen is.

4 Whether they would need to take any linen with them.

5 Whether it has any special features.

6 How much it costs.

SE ALQUILA

Chalet, Guadarrama. 4 dormitorios, 2 cuartos de baño, salón comedor con chimenea, cocina con nevera, lavaplatos y lavadora. Piscina, vista panorámica sierra de Guadarrama. Totalmente amueblado, ropa de cama y baño. Temporada 100.000 ptas. (julio y agosto). Por mes 70.000. Razón Sres Rueda. 223 86 30 (a partir de 6 tarde).

2 Your uncle and aunt are thinking of buying a flat in Spain. They want the flat to have:

– 3 bedrooms

– garage

– entryphone

– fitted wardrobes

1 Which of the features they want are offered in the flats advertised?

2 Do these flats have any other advantages?

3 Where and when can they get more information?

3 Read Sr Lancha's bill and say whether the following statements are true or false.

1 Mr Lancha stayed two nights in the hotel.

2 He had breakfast on the 16th.

3 He made a telephone call.

4 He had to pay VAT.

Hotel PARIS
Calle San Antonio, s/n.
Teléfono 43 70 56
37624 LA ALBERCA
(Salamanca)

GREGORIO LORENZO
N. I. F.: 8.068.879 - L

0382

Sr. D. _Lancha Casahueva_   Habitación núm. _106_

16 Julio 1988	Día _15_ Pesetas	Día _16_ Pesetas	Día Pesetas	Día Pesetas	Día Pesetas	Día Pesetas	Día Pesetas	TOTALES Pesetas
Habitación.	3200							
Desayuno.								3200
Servicio teléfono.		650						650
Servicio de Restaurante	3300							
Servicio Cafetería								3300
TOTALES								
								7150

PRECIOS APLICADOS DE ACUERDO CON LA LEGISLACION VIGENTE

I. V. A. 6 % 429
Total a abonar por el cliente. . 7.579

7699

63

1 You are staying at the *Hotel R. Alfonso X* with your family. Your parents want to know the following:

1 Does the price include service, taxes etc?

2 When is breakfast served? Is it included in the price?

3 What should you do with your room key when you are out?

4 Where can you leave valuables?

5 What do you have to do if you need to ask for something at night?

6 What special services does the hotel offer?

HOTEL R. ALFONSO X

★★★

SALAMANCA (España)

Toro, 64 - Teléfono 21 44 01

C.I.F. A-37002243

Reg. Merc. de Salamanca, tomo 21, folio 184, hoja 306, ins. 1.ª -

FRANCISCO GIL, S.A. -

Habitación   N.º **126**

Ptas. 7290

Servicios incluidos, Impuesto IVA aparte.

Precio noche

Desayuno no incluido

Fecha:

Entrada... 16.7.88.   Firma del cliente

Salida 17. 7. 88

PARA EL CLIENTE

- No olvide **dejar siempre** cerrada la habitación y entregar la llave al conserje al salir.

- Esta Dirección no se hace cargo de objetos que no sean entregados a su custodia.

- No olvide Vd. su pasaporte.

- Desayunos a partir 7,30 mañana. Fruta té, café o chocolate.

- Bar americano.

- Si el cliente se aloja en habitación doble uso individual, la primera noche pagará el 80% del precio de habitación. Si al día siguiente no quiere cambiar a una individual, abonará el 100 por 100 de su precio doble.

- Las habitaciones con salón, apartamentos de tres personas, pagarán lo mismo por una, dos o tres personas, el importe total autorizado. Queda suprimido el Descuento del 20% de los clientes que su estancia sea mayor a dos meses.

- La jornada hotelera terminará a las doce horas. El cliente que no abone a dicha hora la habitación que ocupe, se entenderá que prolonga su estancia un día más, pero si al cliente le ha sido notificado el día de su salida en la presente cartulina, queda obligado también a desalojar la habitación a las 12 horas.

- El precio de la habitación se contará por jornadas o noches.

- Los clientes que no traigan equipaje, pagarán diariamente a su llegada, y si prolongan su estancia más de una noche, lo efectuarán el pago todos los días.

- El Hotel posee servicio de peluquerías.

- A partir de las once de la noche utilice usted el teléfono para pedir cualquier servicio. **Gracias**

2 Find out the following information about the *Parador Nacional 'Enrique II'*

1 When was the castle built?

2 How many rooms does it have?

3 What services does the Parador offer?

4 What does the advert say about the town of Ciudad Rodrigo?

5 What is special about the view from the dining room?

Parador nacional

«Enrique II»

CIUDAD RODRIGO (Salamanca)

**PARADOR NACIONAL
«ENRIQUE II»**

CIUDAD RODRIGO (Salamanca).
Dirección postal: **Plaza del Castillo, n.º 1.**
Dirección telegráfica: PARAL.
Teléfono: 923/46 01 50.
Categoría: TRES estrellas.
Capacidad: 44 plazas, 16 habitaciones dobles y 12 individuales.

Realización • Servicio de Actividades Promocionales. A. T. E.
Impreso por: Mateu Cromo, S. A. Pinto (Madrid)

SECRETARIA DE ESTADO DE TURISMO
DIRECCION GENERAL DE EMPRESAS Y ACTIVIDADES TURISTICAS

Ejemplar gratuito. Venta prohibida. Depósito Legal: M. 15.792-1981

El Castillo-Alcázar de Enrique II de Trastamara fue edificado en el año mil cuatrocientos diez por el ingeniero Lope Arias para su rey. Aquí se encuentra el Parador Nacional, que cuenta con 16 habitaciones dobles y 12 individuales.

El Parador cuenta también con los servicios de cambio de moneda, jardín, calefacción central, aire acondicionado en los salones y comedor, y teléfono y TV en todas las habitaciones. Está clasificado como hotel de tres estrellas.

El Castillo conserva el estilo de la época en que fue construido y los muebles y la decoración del Parador reflejan este estilo.

El Parador se encuentra en la localidad de Ciudad Rodrigo, ciudad amurallada , declarada monumento histórico-artístico. El Parador se halla en el centro de la ciudad, a orillas del río Agueda y sobre una elevada colina. Desde el comedor se disfruta de una vista fantástica sobre el río Agueda, la histórica ciudad y el maravilloso paisaje que se pierde en la lejanía.

7 BASIC Writing

1 You are going to Spain on a school trip. You have to fill in a questionnaire, stating your preferences for accommodation. Write down your responses to a) – f) in Spanish.

a) | Nombre...

b) | Edad................. Sexo.................... Nacionalidad......................

c) | Prefiere alojamiento: (*ver nota 1*)

....

....

d) | Pensión (*ver nota 2*)

....

e) | Fechas

del..............de.......................al ....de..........................

f) | Firma...Fecha....................................

Nota 1; especificar: habitación individual/ a compartir, en hotel, residencia de estudiantes, albergue juvenil.

Nota 2; especificar: pensión completa, pensión media, solo desayuno.

2 You are staying in a hotel in Britain for the weekend. Write a postcard in Spanish to your Spanish penfriend, describing the hotel, the facilities it offers, what there is to do in the area etc.

1 Your parents receive this letter from the *Hotel Residencia Donosti*, in reply to their request for a booking next July. Write a letter back in Spanish, about 100 words long, saying the following:

— Your family does want to book for the last two weeks in June.

— You want a double and a single room, both with bath.

— You'll be having breakfast and evening meals at the hotel.

— You'd like them to send you a programme of the Film Festival.

Hotel Residencia Donosti
Avenida Los Alamos s/n
San Sebastián

13 abril

Muy Sr. mío:

En respuesta a su atenta carta del 12 del corriente, lamento informarle que no nos es posible proporcionarle alojamiento para las fechas del mes de julio que solicita.

Debido al Campeonato de Pelota Vasca que tendrá lugar en nuestra ciudad durante esas fechas, todas nuestras habitaciones están ya reservadas.

Sin embargo, me permito sugerirle, si es posible para usted cambiar la fecha de sus vacaciones, que visiten nuestra ciudad a finales del mes de junio.

Durante el mes de junio tiene lugar en nuestra localidad el famoso Festival de Cine de San Sebastián. Si usted y su familia son aficionados al cine, tendrán oportunidad de asistir a muchas películas, además de otros espectáculos y actividades que tienen lugar al mismo tiempo que el festival.

Si decide usted venir para esas fechas, le aconsejo que nos comunique sus intenciones cuanto antes, para poder asegurarle la reserva.

En espera de sus noticias, le saluda atentamente

Juan Ignacio Goicoechea
Director

2 Your aunt is going to let her house to a Spanish family for the summer. She asks you to write a letter in Spanish to the family, telling them what her house is like. She wants you to mention the following:

— The house is in the country, 2 km away from the village.

— There are buses to the village every 30 minutes. The buses also go to the nearest town, which is 10 km away.

— The house has a living room, a dining room, 3 bedrooms, a bathroom, and a modern kitchen with all appliances (including freezer, dishwasher, washing machine and microwave oven).

— There is no television but it is possible to rent one for the summer.

— There is a garage.

— There is a large garden and beautiful country around the house.

8 BASIC Listening

Services

1 You telephone to find out about transport to the airport, and hear a recorded message twice. Make a note in English of:

— times of buses

— how long it takes to get to the airport.

2 You are staying with your family in a Spanish hotel. They have asked you to find out about the following:

1 What to do about washing clothes.

2 What to do about making phone calls.

3 Whether you can have drinks sent up to the room.

4 Whether you can have breakfast in bed.

Listen to the hotel announcements, which are given twice, and write down in English the information that the family needs.

3 Your parents want to know how to phone Britain. You get a recorded message, which you hear twice. Write down in English what you have to do.

1 A man is at the Tourist Office asking for some information. Make a note in English of the information given by the Tourist Office employee about the following:

a) hotels

b) banks

c) places of interest

d) opening hours of museums

e) booking theatre tickets.

2 A girl wants to hire a car. Listen to the recording and make a note of the following in English:

1 How long she wants the car for.

2 Prices for the cars offered:
a) Citröen BX
b) Seat Ibiza.

3 The one the girl chooses and why.

4 Whether the price includes:
a) mileage
b) insurance
c) tax.

5 When she must return the car.

6 What the assistant asks her to do.

3 Two people are talking about the service offered by the *Farmacias de Guardia*. Listen to their conversation and find out the following information about this service:

1 Times when these chemists are open.

2 Where you can find out about them.

3 What to do if you need a chemist in the middle of the night.

1 *En el estanco*
Work in pairs, taking turns to play each part.

SHOP ASSISTANT	CUSTOMER
¿En qué puedo servirle?	Say you want to buy these two postcards.
Muy bien, las postales cuestan cincuenta y cinco pesetas cada una.	Ask for two stamps for the postcards.
¿Para España o para el extranjero?	Say that they are for Britain.
Aquí tiene, dos sellos de cuarenta y cinco pesetas.	Ask how much it is altogether.
Pues, noventa de los sellos y ciento diez de las postales, doscientos pesetas en total.	Pay and say goodbye.

2 Work in pairs. Take turns in asking each other for the telephone numbers of the services listed here.

A
— radio-controlled taxis

— information about passports

— bus information

B
— information about train tickets

— telephone alarm call

— information about sports

Here is an example:

— ¿Cuál es el teléfono para llamar a una ambulancia?

— Es el dos cincuenta y dos, cuarenta y tres, noventa y cuatro.

Ambulancias	252 43 94
Autobuses interurbanos	468 42 00
Deportes información	464 31 61
Despertador automatico	096
Pasaportes información	222 04 35
Radio- taxi	247 82 00
RENFE	4577 32 41

1 Work in pairs, taking turns to play each part.

CUSTOMER

You want to hire a car for a week.

You would like a Ford Fiesta. Ask about:

– special deals

– prices

– whether there is a charge for mileage

– whether the price includes VAT, insurance etc.

– when you can pick up the car.

CAR-HIRE ASSISTANT

Ask what kind of car.

Answer the customer's questions using the information in the leaflet.

SEMANA COMERCIAL TRIP

negocios sin límites

Al comienzo de una semana, normalmente surge la posibilidad de alquilar un coche para llevar a cabo sus negocios.

En **AUTO TRIP** no queremos distraerle de sus objetivos, por eso le ofrecemos el complemento que mejor le pueda ayudar: nuestra semana **comercial trip.**

GRUPO	MODELOS	COMERCIAL TRIP
A	OPEL CORSA CITY	21.300
B	FORD FIESTA TRIP RENAULT SUPER CINCO	22.900
C	SEAT IBIZA 1.2 OPEL CORSA SWING 1.2	24.800
D	FORD ESCORT 1.3	31.300
E	OPEL KADET 1.3 FORD ORION 1.4	39.600
F	CITROËN BX TRS A/C	47.800

• La tarifa COMERCIAL TRIP va del lunes 09.00 horas a viernes 19.00 horas.

• Kilometraje sin límites.

• Seguros, gasolina e I.V.A. no incluidos.

2 You are flying back to Britain tomorrow, so you phone the airline company to confirm that your flight is leaving as scheduled. Work in pairs, one of you playing the part of the airline attendant. Then exchange roles.

PASSENGER

Ask the attendant whether the flight is leaving according to the details on your ticket.

FLIGHT IB 211 GERONA-LONDON
departs 09.30 a.m.
Passengers should be at the airport
one hour before departure

AIRLINE ATTENDANT

Answer the passenger's questions based on the latest information.

Flight IB 211 will leave on schedule at 09.30 a.m.

Passengers should check in one and a half hours in advance.

8

BASIC
Reading

1 Match each symbol to the description of the service.

A

B

C

Consignas de equipajes 5

Estación de ferrocarril de Atocha.
Estación de ferrocarril de Chamartín.
Estación Sur de Autobuses, Canarias, 17.
Terminal bus Aeropuerto-Colón,
plaza de Colón (subterráneo).

Llamadas urgentes servicios médicos y farmacéuticos 9

Ambulancias. Teléfono: 252 43 94.
Centro Quemados Cruz Roja.
Teléfono: 243 22 19.
Instituto Nacional de Cardiología.
Teléfono: 241 94 69.
Servicio Central de Urgencias Médicas.
Teléfono: 261 61 99.
Urgencias Médicas Seguridad Social

Autobuses interurbanos 2
Estación Sur de Autobuses
de Madrid. Canarias, 17.
Teléfono: 468 42 00.

D

E

F

Transportes 10

Ferrocarril
Red Nacional de los Ferrocarriles
Españoles (RENFE). Central
Teléfono: 457 32 41

Pasaportes 7
Información general. Dirección
General de Seguridad (Puerta del Sol).
Teléfono: 222 04 35.

Embajadas y Consulados 6

Información: Servicio de Protocolo
del Ministerio de Asuntos Exteriores.
Teléfono: 266 52 79.

Otros teléfonos de interés 8
Noticiario de Radio Nacional de España.
Teléfono: 095.
Información Deportiva. Tel. 097.
Servicio Mensafónico. Tel. 221 92 10.
Despertador Automático. Tel. 096.
Mensajes a barcos en alta mar.
Teléfono: 22 11 41.

G

H

Deportes 3

Información. Teléfono: 464 31 61.
Instalaciones. Teléfono: 464 90 08.

Hoteles, apartamentos, pensiones y campings 1

Información sobre establecimientos
hoteleros y campings, puede obtenerse
en las Oficinas de Turismo y en librerías.
Reservas, en agencias de viajes o:

Radio - Taxi 4
Teléfono: 247 82 00.

I

J

8 BASIC Reading

2 What does the *Buenas Noches* service offer? Read the leaflet and say whether these statements are true or false.

1 This service offers things that you can't get when the shops are closed.

2 Amongst the things you can get from the service are:
a) medicines
b) food (including ready-cooked meals) and pet food
c) books
d) drinks, cigarettes.

3 You have to pay 200 pesetas every time you order something.

4 It takes only 15 minutes to deliver what you asked for.

5 You have to be a member to benefit from the service.

BUENAS NOCHES

¿Qué se puede pedir? Prácticamente de todo: Productos de farmacia (medicamentos, alimentos infantiles, biberones, chupetes, etc.), tabacos, cenas, bocadillos, leche, refrescos, vinos, champán, licores, agua mineral, revistas, naipes, bombillas, pilas, enchufes, cables, fusibles, bolígrafos, folios, lapiceros, papel de carta, sobres, carretes de fotos, revelador, fijador, comidas de animales domésticos, artículos de afeitado, imperdibles, sacacorchos, etc.

¿Cuánto cuesta? Sin ningún recargo. Estrictamente a precio de mercado. Con el artículo que pida irá siempre una nota de entrega con el precio.

¿Cuánto tarda? Depende de la zona y el artículo, pero normalmente entre 15 y 40 minutos.

La cuota es de 200 pesetas mensuales, pagaderas por períodos anuales anticipados y a través de su BANCO o CAJA DE AHORROS.

En concepto de entrada se abonarán 200 ptas.

Si le interesa hacerse socio:

– Puede llamarnos a los teléfonos 4238600-4238609.
– Visitarnos o escribirnos enviándonos su nombre, dirección y distrito postal a:

BUENAS NOCHES, San Vicente, 3 - BILBAO-1

1 On arrival in Madrid you are given this leaflet.

1 Who provides the service, and why?

2 What does the service offer?

3 What are the advantages of this service for the tourist?

4 When does it operate?

5 How can you identify the people who provide the service?

DESCUBRE MADRID CON NOSOTROS

El Ayuntamiento de Madrid, a través de su Patronato Municipal de Turismo, vuelve a poner en funcionamiento el servicio "DESCUBRE MADRID CON NOSOTROS" en un intento de acercamiento de la ciudad al visitante.

¿QUE ES "DESCUBRE MADRID CON NOSOTROS"?

Es un servicio de información y orientación turística en la calle. Parejas de jóvenes bien identificados y con amplios conocimientos de Madrid recorren la zona centro de la ciudad, facilitando, en varios idiomas, datos de interés histórico-artísticos, culturales y prácticos al visitante.

¿PARA QUE SE HA CREADO "DESCUBRE MADRID CON NOSOTROS"?

Para completar, ampliar y mejorar el conocimiento de la oferta y atractivos que Madrid encierra de una forma acogedora, directa y personal.

Si buscas un museo, un hotel o un restaurante, dirígete a ellos. Serán tu guía.

Vive Madrid con nosotros.

DURACION Y HORARIO

El servicio funcionará durante los meses de verano.

Horario:	mañanas de 10,00 a 14,00 h.
	tardes de 18,00 a 20,15 h.

COMO Y DONDE LOCALIZARLES

Los jóvenes informadores, vestidos de color amarillo y azul, serán fácilmente localizables por la "**i**" internacional de información y la acreditación del Patronato Municipal de Turismo.

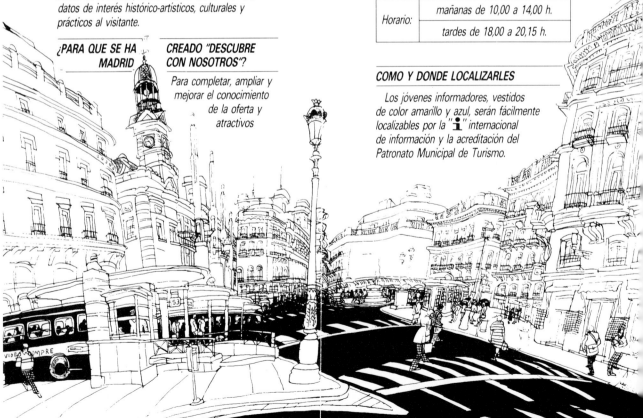

2 Read this leaflet and find out about public libraries in Madrid.

1 What kind of books/periodicals do they have in the libraries?

2 What do you need to become a member?

3 What kind of cultural activities do they organise?

4 What do the children's libraries offer?

5 What are the *Bibliobuses*?

¿CONOCES LAS BIBLIOTECAS POPULARES DE MADRID?

Comunidad de ⬚ Madrid

Madrid cuenta con una importante red de Bibliotecas Populares, de la Comunidad Autónoma, para ofrecer desinteresadamente a cualquiera que lo necesite una amplia variedad de libros de recreo, información o estudio: Diccionarios, enciclopedias, libros de consulta, novelas, obras de teatro, poesías…

Las obras clásicas, las últimas novedades editoriales, y una pequeña colección de los periódicos y las revistas más interesantes, todo esto está a tu disposición en las Bibliotecas Populares. ¿Lo sabías?

¿Por qué no te haces socio?

Si lo deseas, puedes hacerte socio y disfrutar además de otros servicios adicionales. Sólo necesitas:

- Entregar dos fotos.
- Presentar tu D.N.I.
- Rellenar la ficha de inscripción.
- Abonar una cuota anual de 200 pesetas en concepto de gastos de material.

En cualquier Biblioteca Popular puedes realizar los trámites. Ser socio te dará derecho a llevarte prestados a tu casa los libros de la Biblioteca, para tu mayor comodidad.

¿Conoces todos sus servicios?

Las bibliotecas ofrecen varios servicios complementarios:

Actividades Culturales: periódicamente se organizan conferencias, exposiciones, presentaciones de libros, ciclos de cineclub…

Bibliotecas Infantiles: Las Bibliotecas Populares tienen una sección especializada en obras informativas y recreativas para niños y jóvenes, historietas ilustradas, cuentos…

Bibliobuses: Seis autobuses acercan los libros a aquellos barrios que no tienen cerca una biblioteca. Si quieres conocer sus itinerarios y su funcionamiento, pregúntalo en este teléfono.

445 98 45

8 BASIC Writing

Correos y Telégrafos

TELEGRAMA

Destinatario...
Calle o plaza..
Localidad...
....Provincia.................

Texto:

....
....
....
....
....
....

1 While staying in Málaga on holiday you decide to pay a quick visit to your penfriend who lives in Seville. Write a telegram in Spanish, warning him/her of your arrival. Include these details:

— arriving Seville Friday 10.15 p.m. at the bus station

— staying in Seville Saturday and Sunday

— leaving Seville on Monday morning.

2 Your family is exchanging houses with a Spanish family for the summer. Your parents ask you to leave a note in Spanish for the Spanish family, giving information about local services.

This is what you have to mention:

> Buses into town: number 55, every 15 minutes
> Post Office opening hours: 9a.m. to 5 p.m.
> Banks 9.30 a.m. to 3.30 p.m.
> Also open between 4.30p.m and 5.30p.m. on Thursdays.
> Tourist Office is in the High Street for information about places to see, things to do.

3 You want to send a parcel home from Spain. The post office clerk gives you this form.

Copy the form and write down the required details in Spanish.

Nombre ———————	Apellidos ———————
Domicilio ———————	Localidad ———————
Destinatario ———————	Dirección ———————
Contenido ———————	Valor ———————
Firma ———————	Fecha ———————

1 You have been asked by your Spanish teacher to write an information sheet in Spanish about services in your area, to give to the Spanish pupils who are arriving next week as part of the school exchange.

You have to mention the following:

Banks   Which ones are near the school. Opening times. What to do to change foreign currency (they'll need their passports).

Post Offices   Opening times. Location. How much it costs to send a letter to Spain.

Telephones   Public phones. Where to find them. How they work. Cheapest times to phone (between 8 p.m. and 8 a.m. and at weekends).

Other services   Libraries, swimming pools, sports centres etc. Opening times. Location. Prices.

2 Your parents would like to visit the famous wildlife reserve *El Coto de Doñana*, which is in the province of Huelva. Write a letter in Spanish to the Tourist Office in Huelva, asking for the following:

— information about accommodation near the reserve (hotels and campsites)

— details of tours to visit the reserve

— the best time of year to visit it

— the name of the nearest airport, and how to get from the airport to the *Coto*

— a brochure of the area and other places of interest in the province.

PARQUE NACIONAL DE DOÑANA

BASIC Listening 9

Leisure

1 Listen twice to the radio advert and make a note, in English, of the following information:

a) place

b) event

c) times.

2 While staying in Madrid you hear on the radio what is on this week. Make a note in English of the information, which is repeated on the recording. ▷

	Section 1	Section 2	Section 3
What			
Where			
When			
Price			

3 Copy the grid below, then listen to three Spanish people saying what they do in their spare time. You will hear their remarks twice. Put a tick in the appropriate boxes for each person. ▽

	Music	Discos	TV	Cinema	Go out with friends	Read	Sports
Section 1							
Section 2							
Section 3							

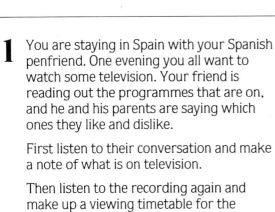

1 You are staying in Spain with your Spanish penfriend. One evening you all want to watch some television. Your friend is reading out the programmes that are on, and he and his parents are saying which ones they like and dislike.

First listen to their conversation and make a note of what is on television.

Then listen to the recording again and make up a viewing timetable for the evening, taking into account everybody's preferences.

2 Your Spanish friend Marisa and another friend, Pedro, are discussing what to do for your last day in Madrid. Listen to their conversation and write down (in English) which of their plans you like best, Marisa's or Pedro's, giving reasons for your choice.

3 You see these two films advertised by the local video library. Your Spanish friend has seen one of them, and she tells you what it is about.

  1 Which of the two films is she talking about?

  2 Write down, in English, some of the details your friend tells you about the film that are *not* mentioned in the advert.

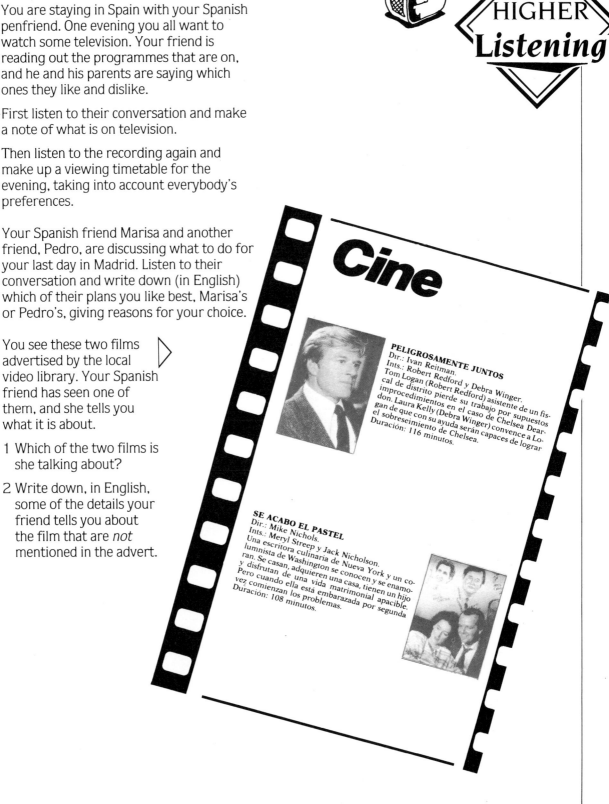

Cine

PELIGROSAMENTE JUNTOS
Dir.: Ivan Reitman.
Ints.: Robert Redford y Debra Winger.
Tom Logan (Robert Redford) asistente de un fiscal de distrito pierde su trabajo por supuestos improcedimientos en el caso de Chelsea Deardon. Laura Kelly (Debra Winger) convence a Logan de que con su ayuda serán capaces de lograr el sobrescimiento de Chelsea.
Duración: 116 minutos.

SE ACABO EL PASTEL
Dir.: Mike Nichols.
Ints.: Meryl Streep y Jack Nicholson.
Una escritora culinaria de Nueva York y un columnista de Washington se conocen y se enamoran. Se casan, adquieren una casa, tienen un hijo y disfrutan de una vida matrimonial apacible. Pero cuando ella está embarazada por segunda vez comienzan los problemas.
Duración: 108 minutos.

9 BASIC Speaking

**Cine
Cinema
Movies**

● **LOS VERANOS DE LA VILLA.** Las siguientes proyecciones tienen lugar, al aire libre, en el **Parque del Retiro** a las 22,15 horas. (Metros Retiro y Atocha).

Día 7: «El Siciliano», «Camorra», «Superman III» y «Vértigo».

Día 8: «La mujer de rojo», «Moros y Cristianos», «El gran enredo», «Cinco semanas en globo» y «Re-po Man».

Día 9: «Hellraiser», «El día de los muertos», «Creepshow», «Birdy» y «D.A.R.Y.L.».

1 Work in pairs.

You want to go to the cinema. Look at the advert and discuss with your partner what film you'd like to go and see, when, and where you'll meet.

Here are some questions and phrases to help you:

— ¿Qué película quieres ver?

— Me gustaría ver. . ./No me gusta ésa.

— ¿Cuándo ponen esa película?

— Esa la ponen el día 8.

— ¿Dónde ponen. . .?

— La ponen en el parque del Retiro.

— ¿Dónde quedamos?

— Quedamos a la entrada del parque/en el café.

— ¿A qué hora empieza la película?

— Empieza a las ocho.

— ¿A qué hora quedamos?

— Quedamos a las siete y cuarto.

2 Your Spanish friend is having a party. You have to phone another friend to tell him/her about the party.

Here are some phrases and questions to help you. Work in pairs, taking turns to play each part.

A
La fiesta es mañana, sábado.

Empieza a las ocho y media.

Van a venir todos los amigos del colegio.

Tienes que traer algo de música y algo para beber.

B
¿A qué hora empieza?

¿Quién va a ir a la fiesta?

¿Hay que traer algo?

1 Make a recording of how you spend your free time, to send to your Spanish penfriend. These questions will help you to prepare the recording.

— ¿Qué te gusta hacer en tu tiempo libre?

— ¿Qué tipo de música prefieres? ¿Qué grupos/cantantes te gustan más?

— ¿Qué hay en tu ciudad para los jóvenes?

— ¿Ves mucho la televisión? ¿Qué tipo de programas prefieres?

— ¿Qué deportes practicas? ¿Hay muchas facilidades para hacer deporte en tu ciudad?

— ¿Tienes algún hobby? ¿Y tus amigos? ¿Comparten tus aficiones?

2 Work in pairs.

Below are the opinions of two Spanish teenagers about whether it is better to watch a film on video or to go to the cinema. Discuss with your partner the advantages and disadvantages of both arguments, and say who you agree with.

Yo prefiero ir al cine a ver las películas en vídeo, porque la pantalla grande es mucho más impresionante. Además, al estar a oscuras en el cine pones más atención y es casi como si estuvieras dentro de la historia de la película. En tu casa, en una pantalla de televisión no es lo mismo, no se puede comparar con la emoción de ir al cine .

Yo prefiero el vídeo, porque es mucho más cómodo que ir al cine. Tienes muchas más películas para elegir y las ves en tu casa tan tranquilo, cuando quieres. Al cine, a veces vas y no hay entradas y te tienes que volver a casa. Además el vídeo sale más barato, porque por el precio del alquiler, ve la película toda la familia, y la puedes ver las veces que quieras.

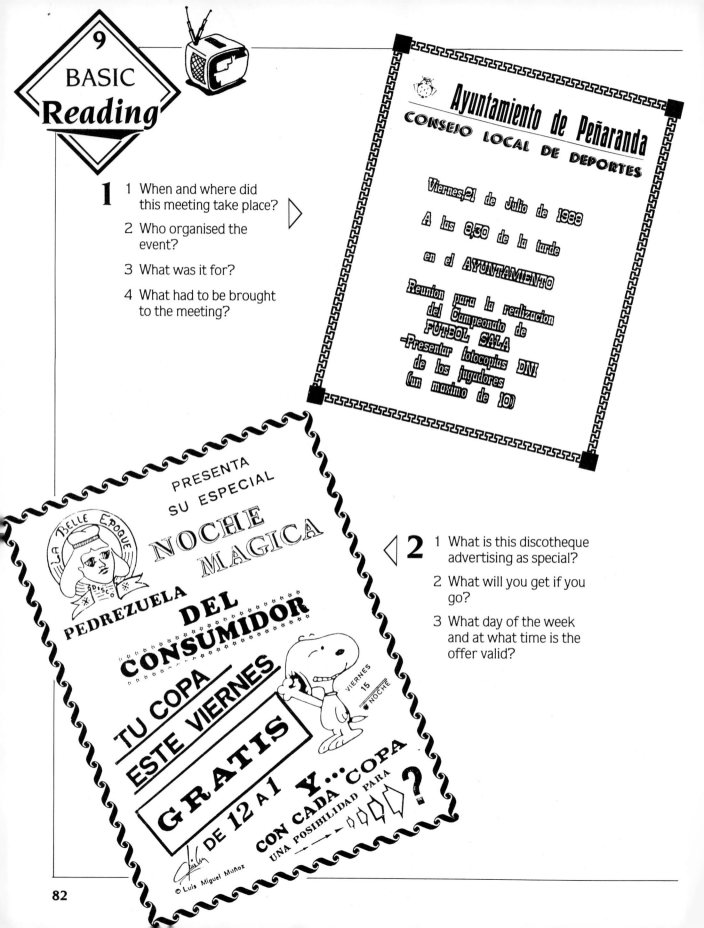

1

1 When and where did this meeting take place?

2 Who organised the event?

3 What was it for?

4 What had to be brought to the meeting?

Ayuntamiento de Peñaranda
CONSEJO LOCAL DE DEPORTES

Viernes, 21 de Julio de 1988

A las 8,30 de la tarde

en el AYUNTAMIENTO

Reunion para la realizacion del Campeonato de FUTBOL SALA -Presentar fotocopias DNI de los jugadores (un maximo de 10)

PRESENTA
SU ESPECIAL

NOCHE MAGICA

LA BELLE EPOQUE

PEDREZUELA DEL CONSUMIDOR

TU COPA ESTE VIERNES

GRATIS

DE 12 A 1 Y... COPA

CON CADA COPA
UNA POSIBILIDAD PARA

VIERNES 15 NOCHE

© Luis Miguel Muñoz

2

1 What is this discotheque advertising as special?

2 What will you get if you go?

3 What day of the week and at what time is the offer valid?

3
1 How much does it cost to get into the Safari Park?

2 Mention five places that you can go to in the park.

3 How can you get a 50% discount?

4 Until when does this offer apply?

SAFARI MADRID
RESERVA EL RINCON

ALDEA DEL FRESNO
Tels. 862 08 11
862 06 57

RR

PRECIOS SIN DESCUENTO
- PRECIO ADULTOS 700 PTAS.
- PRECIO NIÑOS 500 PTAS.

PASE UN DIA INOLVIDABLE CON SU FAMILIA VISITANDO EL SAFARI DE MADRID. LE OFRECEMOS VISITAR:
* EL SAFARI
* LA MINI-RESERVA
* EXHIBICION DE RAPACES
* VISITA AL REPTILARIO
* EXHIBICION DE REPTILES
Y ADEMAS:
- PISCINAS
- TOBOGANES ACUATICOS
- RESTAURANTE (10 % DCTO.)

TODO CON EL 50 % DE DESCUENTO

SOLO HASTA EL 31 DE JULIO

OBTENGA UN 50 % DE DESCUENTO PRESENTANDO ESTE RECORTE

4 You want to go and see this concert. Find out the following information:

a) date and time

b) place

c) where to get tickets

d) what to do to get cheaper tickets.

MECANO

SABADO 16 DE SEPTIEMBRE
10 NOCHE
AUDITORIO MADRID-CASA DE CAMPO MAGIC

ENTRADAS A LA VENTA EN CENTROS DE
1200 Ptas VENTA ANTICIPADA
1500 Ptas DIA DEL CONCIERTO
AUTOBUSES: 31,39,65,36 NOCTURNO 8 METRO LAGO

HIGHER
Reading

1 Your parents want to know what is on Spanish television tonight. Look at the TV programme schedule and make a note in English about the following types of programme, and their times:

a) the news

b) soap operas

c) sport

d) the weather

e) films

f) TV series.

TVE-1

07,55: BUENOS DIAS.
08,30: TELEDIARIO MATINAL.
09,00: POR LA MAÑANA.
De 10,00 a 10,50: ■ CUATRO HOMBRES PARA EVA.
De 11,50 a 12,40: ■ DINASTIA.

Blake consigue numerosas concesiones en una de las zonas más importantes del mundo: el mar del sur de China. Firmados los contratos, se dispone a regresar a Dénver.

«Dinastía»

13,00: LOS OSOS BERENSTAIN. «El hermano oso es estrella del fútbol».

El oso cachorro sueña con presentarse a las pruebas de fútbol del equipo universitario, pero parece que, debido a su poca talla, tendrá que olvidarlo por el momento.

13,30: 3×4.

Julia Otero («3×4»)

15,00: TELEDIARIO.
15,35: ■ FAMA.
16,30: UN VERANO TAL CUAL.
18,00: AVANCE TELEDIARIO.
18,05: LA LINTERNA MAGICA.
19,30: DICCIONARIO DE LA SALUD.

(Repetición: Sábado 9, a las 09,45.)

«Fiebre».

Dirección, guión y presentación: Ramón Sánchez-Ocaña.
Realización: Pedro Pérez Oliva.

Tras un repaso del sistema regulador de temperatura, se analiza a qué llamamos fiebre y se dan una serie de consejos para poner en práctica en caso de fiebre.

Ramón Sánchez-Ocaña («Diccionario de la salud»)

20,00: ■ MASH. «¿Quién lo sabía?».

El coronel Potter comunica a todo el personal del Mash la muerte de la enfermera teniente Carpenter, ocurrida al pisar una mina. Su fama de fría y distante se desvanece al encontrar un diario entre sus objetos personales.

20,30: TELEDIARIO.
21,00: EL TIEMPO.
21,15: CARA A CARA.
22,30: □ ◆ VIERNES CINE.

«Encuentros en la tercera fase» (ver columna lateral).

00,55: TELEDIARIO.
01,15: TELEDEPORTE.

2 You would like to spend a day in a *parque de agua*, but you don't know which one to choose.

Here is some information about two parks. Write down in English what each of them offers, under the following headings:
— water attractions
— swimming pools
— games
— food/drink
— opening hours
— price.

El acuático
PARQUE ACUATICO DE MADRID

Pasa un día entero a lo grande, sin parar de divertirte, de refrescarte, de disfrutar. Ven con quien quieras, con tus amigos, con tus padres, con tus hijos... Hay diversiones para todos. En el Acuático puedes también comer y beber, comprar, y no parar en todo el día, o tirarte al sol o a la sombra y pasar el día sin moverte. Lo que quieras. Lo que busques lo encontrarás en el Acuático. Ven. ¡Mójate!

Instalaciones:
1 Lago de 7.000 m² de superficie al que tienen acceso:

4 Toboganes zig-zag.
2 Toboganes espirales.
6 Pistas blandas o foam.
8 Toboganes multipistas.
2 Kamikazes.
4 toboganes infantiles.

Juegos:
Resbalones, setas, dinos.
Piscina de chapoteo super infantil con toboganes.
(Niños menores de 3 años).
1 Piscina de olas.
(1.600 m² de superficie).

Otras instalaciones:
17.000 m² de praderas.
1 Self service (con sombras).
2 Kioscos (bares) con terrazas y sombras.

1 Pic-nic.
Alquiler de tumbonas.
Tienda de souvenirs y accesorios.
Pizzería.

PARQUES DE AGUA

■ **AQUOPOLIS.**
Villanueva de La Cañada. Tel. 815 69 11. Abierto de diez de la mañana a ocho de la tarde. Precio: 1.300 para los adultos y 900 los niños.

■ **EL ACUATICO.**
Carretera de Barcelona, km. 15. Tel. 673 01 13. Abierto de diez de la mañana a ocho de la tarde. Precio: 1.200 pesetas para los adultos en días festivos y 1.000 en días laborables. Los niños, 900 pesetas.

Si quieres dejarte llevar por el agua mientras te tomas algo, disfruta de esta atracción en Aquópolis. Te pides algo en el bar, te sientas en uno de los comodísimos sillones inflables y a disfrutar mientras una suave corriente te lleva sobre el agua. Pruébalo, es de lo más especial... y relajante. Además, en Aquópolis podrás encontrar todo tipo de atracciones acuáticas para todas las edades.

Desde toboganes de todos los tipos y formas hasta divertidas piscinas con juegos. También tenemos pizzerías, heladerías, restaurantes, barbacoas y todo lo necesario para que pases un día aquacionante. Prohibido introducir latas y objetos de vidrio en el recinto del Parque. Venta de entradas en Viajes Vincit y en el propio Parque.

aquopolis

AQUOPOLIS ES LA DIVERSION MAS GORDA DEL VERANO. SEGURO. En Villanueva de la Cañada, a 25 Km. de Madrid. Abierto todos los días de 10 a 20 horas. Autobuses gratis todos los días desde la Plaza de España.

9 BASIC Writing

1 You are in Spain on a school exchange. Your exchange partner has been keeping a diary of the things you have been doing together, in English, because he/she wants to practise.

Write *your* diary for the past week in Spanish.

Lunes

Viernes

Martes

Sábado

Miercoles

Domingo

Jueves

Invitación

....
....
....
....
....
....
....
....
....
....

2 Your Spanish penfriend is coming to stay with you, and will be here for your birthday. Write an invitation to your birthday party in Spanish for your friend.

3 Do a survey of the favourite television programmes of members of your family, or a group of friends. Use a grid like the one below.

Documentales	Programas deportivos	Programas musicales	Teleseries	Películas

Write a short report of your findings in Spanish.

1 Look again at task 2 on page 81. Write a summary in Spanish of your opinion about the cinema versus video argument.

2 This is what some Spanish teenagers wrote about the leisure facilities in their area:

> *En mi pueblo casi no hay nada que hacer para los jóvenes. Sólo ir al club de jóvenes, pero allí tampoco hay mucho que hacer: ping-pong, televisión y el bar. De vez en cuando hay un baile o una discoteca, pero en general es muy aburrido.*

> *En mi barrio tenemos un polideportivo genial, y también hay muchas discotecas y cafeterías, pero a mí lo que me gustaría es tener un cine. Ahora, si quieres ir al cine te tienes que ir al centro, y se tarda por lo menos una hora.*

> *En mi opinión, lo que falta aquí es un polideportivo. Hay cantidad de discotecas, bares y cafeterías, pero de deporte sólo tenemos la piscina, y casi nunca voy porque siempre está llena de gente.*

How does this compare with where you live? Write an account in Spanish of the leisure facilities in your area, and give your opinion as to whether or not they are adequate.

Everyday problems

1 Listen to six people
explaining why they are
not feeling well. You will
hear them twice. In which
section (1–6) is each of
the following ailments
mentioned?

a) toothache

b) stomach ache

c) headache

d) sore throat and a cough

e) backache

f) aching legs.

2 Your father has lost his wallet. It is a brown
leather wallet and it contained 2500
pesetas, some photos and some credit
cards.

You hear an announcement in the hotel. It
is repeated. Has your father's wallet been
found? If so, write down which is your
father's: 1, 2 or 3.

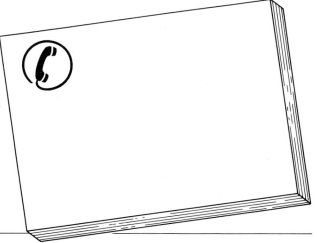

3 You are staying with your Spanish friend in
Almería. The phone rings when you are
alone in the house. You will hear the
message twice. Write it down in English.

1 You are at a railway station in Spain and you overhear a conversation. Listen to it and answer the following questions in English.

   1 Where is the man going?

   2 Why did he miss the train?

   3 Are there other trains today for that destination?

   4 Which train does the railway attendant recommend and why?

   5 What service does that train have?

2 A customer is returning a coffee maker to the shop because it is faulty. Listen to her conversation with the shop assistant, and answer these questions in English.

   1 What is wrong with the coffee maker?

   2 What does the assistant suggest?

   3 What does the customer want?

3 While you are staying in Spain with your Spanish friend, his camera stops working. You go with him to the shop where he bought it. Listen to the conversation and find out:

   1 What is wrong with the camera.

   2 Whether the film in the camera will be spoiled.

   3 How much it will cost to have it repaired.

   4 When it will be ready.

10
BASIC
Speaking

1 You have got a cold and you go to the chemist to buy something for it. Work in pairs, one of you playing the part of the pharmacist. Then exchange roles.

PHARMACIST	CUSTOMER
¿En qué puedo servirle?	Ask if he/she has anything for a cold.
Sí, hay muchas cosas para el catarro. ¿Le duele la garganta?	Yes, you have a sore throat and also a cough.
Estas pastillas van muy bien para el catarro.	Ask if they are good for the cough too.
Para la tos tengo este jarabe.	Say you'll take the tablets and the cough mixture. Ask how often you have to take them.
Tiene que tomar dos pastillas cuatro veces al día, y el jarabe, una cucharada cada cuatro horas.	Ask how much it is, pay and say goodbye.

2 You are staying in Spain with your penfriend. Tonight you had been invited to a party, but your friend is not feeling well and you think you should stay with him/her.

Phone the friend who had invited you to the party to say that you are not going. Work in pairs, one of you playing the part of the Spanish friend. Then exchange roles.

A	B
Greet your friend.	¡Hola! Vienes esta tarde ¿verdad?
Say that you can't go to the party.	¡No me digas! ¿Por qué?
Explain that your friend is ill.	Pues es una pena, porque va a estar genial.
Say that you are sorry to miss it.	Bueno, no te preocupes, seguro que habrá más fiestas.
Thank your friend and say goodbye.	

1 *En la oficina de objetos perdidos*

You have just arrived at your hotel in Alicante when you realise that you have lost one of your travelling bags.

Work in pairs, taking turns to play each part.

LOST PROPERTY OFFICIAL	TOURIST
Ask if you can help.	Say you have lost a bag. You think you may have left it at the station.
Ask the person's name and address.	Give your name and the address of your hotel.
Ask for a description of the bag and its contents.	Say it is a navy blue plastic bag, containing clothes (trousers, T-shirts, underwear, socks etc.), some books (including your Spanish dictionary) and toilet articles.
Say that you don't have the bag.	Ask what to do next.
Tell the person to phone tomorrow, between 10 a.m. and 1p.m.	

2 Your parents' car is not running very well. You have to tell the Spanish garage attendant what is wrong and ask when it will be ready. Work in pairs, one of you playing the part of the garage attendant.

Here are some phrases to help you:

— ¿De qué marca es el coche?

— ¿Qué le pasa al coche?   — Los frenos no funcionan bien/El motor hace un ruido muy raro.

— ¿Cuándo lo puede arreglar?   — Estará listo esta tarde/mañana/dentro de 2 días.

— ¿Cuánto va a costar?   — Ahora no le puedo decir. Tengo que ver qué le pasa.

— ¿Puede llamar por teléfono esta tarde/mañana por la mañana?

— ¿Me deja las llaves del coche, por favor?

10 BASIC Reading

1 Your Spanish penfriend was left alone in your house while you were away for the day visiting your grandmother. Everything seems to have gone wrong in your absence. She is out at the moment, but she has left you all these messages. Read the messages and write down in English what happened.

(a)

¡Lo siento! Dejé el pescado que había comprado para la cena en la mesa de la cocina y el gato se lo comió.

(b)

¡Perdón! Estaba limpiando el polvo en el cuarto de estar y se me cayó el jarrón azul y blanco y se rompió.

(c)

No sé que pasa con la TV, pero no funciona. Se ve bien la imagen, pero no se oye nada. Yo no he hecho nada, de verdad.

(d)

Llamó Peter. Que no puede ir al cine contigo mañana. Tiene la gripe y se siente fatal.

Y sobre todo...... ¡Cuidado con el sol!

Para evitar el peligro de la insolación y conseguir un bronceado perfecto, te recomendamos lo siguiente:

1   Toma el sol poco a poco. El primer día, nada más que cinco minutos y cada día un poquito más.
2   Utiliza cremas con filtro solar. El número del filtro depende del tipo de piel.
3   Los primeros días, evita tomar el sol entre las 12 y las 4 de la tarde. Es cuando pega más fuerte.
4   Después de tomar el sol, ponte una loción aftersun, para calmar e hidratar la piel.
5   No te pongas nunca colonia o desodorante si vas a tomar el sol.

2 You find this article in a Spanish magazine. Make a note of the five pieces of advice it gives you on how to avoid sunstroke and get a good suntan.

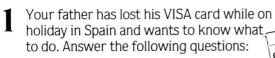

1

Your father has lost his VISA card while on holiday in Spain and wants to know what to do. Answer the following questions:

1 When and where can you get help from this service if you lose your card?

2 How much money can you get straight away?

3 When could this be particularly useful?

4 How long will it take for a replacement card to be issued?

5 What other help does *Visa Oro* provide?

6 What do you have to do to make use of this service?

2

You are looking forward to the arrival of your penfriend Marisa who is due to arrive next week. You get this letter from her, telling you that she cannot come. Find out what the problem is:

1 Where was she when the accident happened?

2 How did it happen?

3 What did her friends do?

4 Why can't she come to England?

5 Why is she fed up?

CENTRO VISA DE SERVICIO AL VIAJERO

Una de las ventajas exclusivas de la Tarjeta VISA ORO es la de tener permanentemente a su disposición un servicio de asistencia internacional para situaciones de emergencia. A él debe usted acudir especialmente en caso de desaparición de su tarjeta.

Cualquier día de la semana, a cualquier hora, en cualquier lugar del mundo, el centro VISA de Servicio al Viajero le prestará ayuda inmediata mediante:

• La gestión de un anticipo en efectivo de hasta 5.000* dólares en moneda local, como dinero de emergencia, que puede resultarle especialmente práctico si, además de su tarjeta, sufre la pérdida de su documentación o equipaje.

• La reposición urgente de su tarjeta en el plazo más breve posible (generalmente no superior a cuarenta y ocho horas).

• El envío de un mensaje urgente a su familia o empresa.

Para ello, telefonee al Centro VISA de Servicio al Viajero a uno de estos números:

España (Madrid)	(91) 435 24 45
Inglaterra, desde cualquier lugar del mundo (Londres)	938 10 31
Estados Unidos, desde territorio continental	(800) 336 - 3386
Estados Unidos, desde los demás lugares	(703) 556 - 8878
Alemania (Frankfurt)	29 51 78
Austria (Viena)	54 11 46
Bélgica (Aalst)	(53) 77 65 93
Dinamarca (Copenhague)	19 28 28

*Sujeto a lo dispuesto en la legislación vigente en materia de divisas.

¡Hola!

Te escribo con muy malas noticias. Tengo que decirte que no puedo ir a verte como habíamos planeado. Verás lo que me ha pasado.

El domingo pasado estaba en la piscina con unos amigos, cuando de repente me picó una abeja en el pie. Con el susto y el dolor me resbalé y me caí. Intenté ponerme de pie pero no pude, me dolía la pierna muchísimo. Mis amigos me llevaron al hospital en un coche y el resultado es que me he roto una pierna y la tengo que tener escayolada seis semanas. No te puedes imaginar el disgusto que tengo. Aquí estoy, en pleno verano, super incómoda, porque la escayola molesta y más con el calor tan terrible que hace. No puedo salir a ningún sitio y, por supuesto, no puedo ir a la piscina. Lo peor de todo es que no puedo ir a verte, con las ganas tan grandes que tenía. Así que ya ves. Siento mucho estropear tus planes de verano, pero así es la vida. Escríbeme pronto para animarme un poco.

Un abrazo de

Marisa

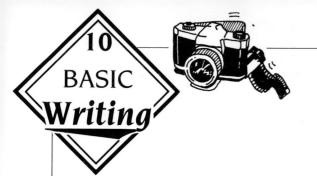

10 BASIC Writing

1 You are staying in Spain on a school exchange. After spending a day at your partner's school, you realise that you have lost your wallet. Write a notice for the school noticeboard, describing the wallet and its contents, and giving your name and address or phone number.

Use this notice that is already on the board as a model.

PERDIDO

Bolso azul marino, de plástico.
Contiene: pantalones cortos azules, camiseta blanca y zapatillas de deporte.

Llamar a: Maite Arnaiz. 233 45 21 por las tardes

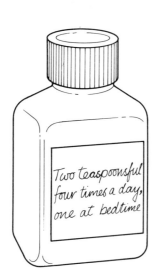

Two teaspoonsful four times a day, one at bedtime

2 Your Spanish friend, who is staying with you, has been to the doctor because he/she was not feeling well. Your friend has got some medicine, but is not very sure how much to take or how often.

Translate the instructions on the label into Spanish for your partner.

3 Your penfriend's parents have just phoned while your friend was out. They can't go to meet him/her at the airport, because grandmother is ill and they are going to stay with her. Your friend has to get a taxi from the airport and go to his/her aunt's house.

Write the message in Spanish for your friend.

1 After returning from a holiday in Santander, your mother realises that she has left her favourite handbag in the hotel where you stayed.

Write a letter in Spanish to the hotel, describing the bag, saying where she left it and asking if it is possible to send it to you. Say in the letter that you are prepared to pay for the cost of sending it.

2 You had a terrible meal in a Spanish restaurant. The food was awful and the waiter got the order wrong. The service was slow and the waiter was rude. You decide to take advantage of the *Hoja de reclamaciones* to which all customers are entitled.

Write your complaint in Spanish. ▷

HOJA DE RECLAMACIONES

Nombre y dirección del establecimiento
....
....

Nombre y dirección del cliente
....
....

Reclamación:
....
....
....
....
....
....

Firma................Fecha..........

3 Your Spanish penfriend has written to tell you that he/she has had an operation and has had to stay in hospital for a week. You decide to send him/her a present and a letter to cheer him/her up. Write the letter to your friend in Spanish.

Acknowledgements

Cartoons by Terry Rogers, Linden Artists

Diagrams by RDL Artset

Photographs by permission of:
Universal Pictorial Press and Agency Ltd p9; Anthony Langham pp15, 39; Barnaby's Picture Library pp28, 61 (top right), 66, 87 (top right, bottom right), 89; ZEFA Picture Library p33; Landscape Only p38; Laurence Kimpton p77; Sally and Richard Greenhill p87

Cover: David Simson top, bottom right; Laurence Kimpton bottom left

All other photographs by the author

Sources of other illustrations:
Popcorn p9; ABC p9; El Corte Inglés pp16, 46, 60; Colegio Mayor Guadalupe pp18, 19; Diario 16 pp26, 55; Ayuntamiento de Madrid p27; RENFE pp29, 34; Cambio 16 p36; Catalunya, Direccio General de Turisme p37; Grupo Digsa p44; Las Horcas Restaurant p45; El País pp45, 84; En Madrid, Patronato Municipal de Turismo pp46, 71, 72, 74, 75, 80; AMA p52; Guía de Madrid p53; Restaurante El Vagón, La Nueva Máquina, El Soto, Sivagami, Ristorante Piccolo p54; Tele Indescrita p55; Castillo del Miramar p62; Hotel París p63; Hotel Rey Alfonso X p64; Instituto Nacional de Promoción del Turismo p65; Oficina Central de Correos p70; Buenas Noches p73; Bibliotecas Populares de Madrid p75; RONDA (Iberia) p79; Diez Minutos p84; Banco de Bilbao p93

Every effort has been made to locate and contact the source of each illustration. We will be pleased to rectify any omissions in future printings.